THE WOMEN'S LAND ARMY
was excluded from marching in the Remembrance Day Parade at the Cenotaph until 2000, when it was included – to march at the back. Land Girls received no gratuities at the end of the war – and on disbandment, they returned **DIGGING FOR MEMORIES:** *their uniforms and received no* **The Women's Land Army** *civvy clothes and precious* **in Cornwall** *little thanks. They were awarded no service medals, as were the other three women's services, yet all the recruitment service posters showed the FOUR women's services, ATS, WRENS, WAAFS and the WLA, marching shoulder to shoulder under the flag, telling us that* OUR COUNTRY NEEDED US.

This publication is part of a series of social research reports about British women and their educational achievement and occupational activity. Others in this series include:

The English Countrywoman 1900-2000
by Dr Mary Casling

Educating Nurses in Scotland 1950-2000
by Dr Rosemary Weir

Balmaidens, The History of Women Mineworkers in Devon & Cornwall
by Lynne Mayers

Additional titles forthcoming.

DIGGING FOR MEMORIES

The Women's Land Army in Cornwall

"The main thing I remember from the Land Army
during World War II was the way it gave me
a whole new outlook on life."
- Ann Foreman, Hayle

Edited by Melissa Hardie

Based on interviews by Diana Ayres & Angie Butler

The Hypatia Trust
Trevelyan House
Penzance, Cornwall
2006

This edition of *Digging for Memories: The Women's Land Army in Cornwall* is published in 2006 by

The Hypatia Trust
Trevelyan House
16 Chapel Street
Penzance, Cornwall, TR18 4AW
01736 366597

A catalogue record for this book is available from the British Library.

ISBN 1-872229-64-6

Book design by Donna J. Anton

Cover photograph: Ann Skewes *nee* Morgan.
Photograph on page vii: Pat Peters *nee* Davis.

Support Funding for the Digging for Memories Project:

Home Front Recall
Heritage Lottery Fund

The Hypatia Trust

Healthy Living Initiative
Small Grants Fund

Community Chest
(Penwith Community
Development Fund)

Printed in the United Kingdom
by R Booth Ltd
Penryn, Cornwall

3rd Reprint

Contents

COOL GRANDMA

What did you do in the War, Grandma?
We're learning about it at school.
Were you a WAAF or an ATS or a Wren?
They looked so cool.

Haven't they taught you about the land,
How the men had to go and fight,
How thousands of girls, from cities and towns,
Became farmers overnight?

We were the Women's Land Army,
Eighty thousand strong.
We worked all hours in the heat and the cold,
Each day was hard and long.

We dug the ditches, milked the cows,
Brought in the harvest grain.
Collected the eggs and killed the rats!
We braved the wind and rain.

A Cinderella Army,
We weren't asked to the Ball.
But aching backs and weary limbs
Were remembered by us all.

Yet through the hardship and the toil
We did our very best.
A job well done was our reward,
And never mind the rest.

That's what we did in the War, child,
So tell your friends at school.
They won't see us in the Big Parade,
But Land Girls? We were cool!

Hilda Gibson, 1999

Threshing in winter at Cullarian Farm, St Erth
(photo courtesy of Betty Clark)

INTRODUCTION

Digging for Memories

When a former Mayor of Penzance, Ruth Simpson, casually mentioned that she had been talking recently with a former Land Girl and how fascinating her memories were, our interest was immediately piqued. Ruth suggested we might like to interview remaining Land Girls here in Cornwall, because "we are running out of time to capture true-life stories." Indeed, within a fortnight of gathering our Land Army study team together, one of us was attending the funeral of Evelyn James (1919-2005).

Evelyn met her future husband, Desmond James, because she took a 14-hour train journey to Penzance from her home in Blackburn, Lancashire, to join the Land Army. She was assigned to the Tomlin Bros. at Polgoon, working there throughout the war. Attending St Mary's Church, where Desmond was a server, they met and later married when he returned from Royal Navy war service. Eve, as she was known, remained for the rest of her life in Cornwall, where she was much liked and described as "loving wife, mother and grandmother." Desmond, who died in 2002, worked for many years with Lloyd's Bank, was a player of rugby, and later president of the Penzance-Newlyn club.

Though she was not to be directly part of our Oral History Project, in Eve we found a thread of the whole fabric to emerge from wartime memories: disruption, movement, travel, hard work, joy and laughter, tragedy and new lives. The special effect that this "new blood" had in and on Cornwall is well told by Mary Quick, in her own account of the life of her friend Betty Williams Berriman, extracts from which are included from her 1995 (50th anniversary) article in the *St Ives Times & Echo*. A wonderfully evocative report series in three parts was loaned to us, first published in 1980 in the *Middleton Guardian*, Lancashire, written by Elizabeth Nicholls. Entitled "A Blackley Girl in Cornwall," this series of articles based on her diaries kept throughout the war, has been steadily employed over the 60 years since as a basis for talks and gatherings in commemoration of the Land Army.

Betty Williams Berriman (1994)

Cornwall is a microcosm and has its own wartime stories to tell, as do other counties, each of which were organised separately, each having its own Organising Secretariat and local representatives. Lois Pulford, writing to us from Wales, where she now lives, brings that special Cornish flavour into her brief narrative. Unique to each woman, we wanted to hear the personal voices of the Land Army telling us what had proved life-changing and life-sustaining to them. And, we wanted to speculate on how the influx helped to change the face of Cornwall, as the world wars have changed the face of the Europe as we know it today.

The first notice of the Land Army Oral History Project launched in Cornwall by the Hypatia Trust was published in county-wide newspapers in early spring of 2005. Under the title "Looking for Land Girls," the press articles asked their readers to alert "your mothers, your sisters, your cousins and your aunts" in good Gilbert & Sullivan fashion, anyone who would share their stories of life in the Land Army in Cornwall during World War II. The response was tremendous, and surprisingly so. Close to a hundred women, their families and friends (some being sons and husbands of Land Army girls) have been in touch with us, and some from as far afield as Canada, the United States, New Zealand and Australia. The Cornish network is obviously alive and well, and the 60th anniversary of the end of World War II has proved a fertile time for "digging for memories."

This commemorative book was the objective, and a brief documentary video-film. With the help of a grant from the Home Front Recall (supported by the Heritage Lottery Fund and the Big Lottery Fund) and the Penwith Community Development Fund, the work could be expanded to become an educational and social project, reuniting those women remaining within the county with each other, recording the stories they have to tell, and distilling the record to keep for all time. Our special thanks are due to Paul Green, Social Exclusion officer of the Cornwall

THE LAND GIRLS PROJECT

Rural Community Council, for his expert help with preparation of the applications we made for financial support. Additional financial help from the Healthy Living Initiative Small Grants Fund, especially Susie Hall, enabled the design of a permanent data collection instrument from which a Land Girls Data Base of Information has been evolved.

Immediate offers of help were forthcoming. Initial photographs were shared from the Cornwall Centre Collection, Redruth, through the good offices of the D-Day Voices Project headed up previously by Chris Hibbert of Trebah Gardens. John Pollard made contact and offered to share "Marazion Memories" information relevant to the Land Army. Charlotte Chadwick of Penwith District Council offered immediate help with planning for events to be held in relation to Armistice and Memorial Day celebrations. One of our project team, Llyn Aubrey, made a study visit to the Imperial War Museum in London, obtaining their recommended reading list of books about the Women's Land Army, and their keen interest in our Project and the book that would emerge. Another of our team, Angie Butler, together with Nickie Carlyon, designed a logo for the Cornish Land Army Project, and supervised the production of our team stationery, aided by the computer skills of Dave Philp. Peter Waverly, the Elizabeth Treffry Collection curator of the Hypatia Trust, carried out an intensive newspaper search, at the Cornwall Centre, Redruth, for Cornish releases related to the Land Army from 1939 through 1950 when it was disbanded nationally.

All of the above information sources are gratefully acknowledged, and also the help given along the way by numerous individuals providing cuttings, contacts, photographs, letters, badges, posters and even two original sets of Land Army dungarees, which must have escaped re-cycling (most were returned and made into other garments). The media have been especially helpful, not only aiding us in the search for Land Girls, but recounting and displaying some of the interviews and tea parties that have been arranged. They have also generously given their permission for reprinting historical articles and photographs from their archives. The *West Briton,* the *Cornishman,* and the *Western Morning News* have carried regular reports, and ITV and BBC Radio Cornwall have carried items at some length. Thanks for venues offered by the public libraries in St Austell, Helston and Truro, providing a gathering point for some of the interviews that could not always be held in individual homes. Special thanks to Janet Spargo of the Helston Folk Museum for the provision of a large number of recommended menus issued by the Ministry of Food in 1945, and to June Johnstone for her Cornish Recipe book. Trevelyan House in Chapel Street, Penzance, has proved a very comfortable home for the project as a whole, and for some of the West Cornwall interviews and meetings.

The video team, headed by Llyn Aubrey, included Daniel Kadi, and worked under the guidance of Barbara Santi, who became the producer of the documentary film, and their expertise is much appreciated. Nickie Carlyon assisted with promotional aspects and Coreen Brown with administrative work. Angie Butler was the Events Leader for the team and organised marvellous commemorative exhibitions and parades at St John's Hall, Penzance, at the St Just VE/VJ Day Celebrations in Penwith, and not least for the Cornish VE-VJ Day 60th Commemorations Tea Party in Truro. Diana Ayres and Angie Butler have conducted the taped interviews, both individually in private homes and at joint tea parties arranged for the purpose, then transcribed these for the historical archive. Melissa Hardie has edited this book, based on the recordings, transcriptions, and other historical material made available by the Land Girls. The educational package developed from the project will be available on loan from the Hypatia Trust, and from the Cornwall Centre, Redruth. It can be borrowed for special events, schools, and exhibitions by appointment. Truly a team effort, the "home team" is grateful for all the kindnesses and help received.

Most of all, we want to express our gratitude to the Land Girls who have allowed us to include their stories within the book and documentary. They dug for victory; we have dug again for their memories. We have listed those women on the Honour Roll at the back of the book, with whom we have had contact, either directly or indirectly, through written reports rendered by husbands and families. Some women read about the project in *Saga Magazine* (November 2005) and made contact almost as the editing of the book was complete. Hence, everything that we have received could not be included in the final production, but we will be able to keep these records in our data collection for the future use of families and researchers. No story will be wasted.

We have been met with such interest, good humour and kindness. Some Land Army girls who did not work in Cornwall during the war period, nevertheless live here now. And we have included some of their memories too. We have to say thanks for the hard and heavy work they did, alongside the women who served in the other women's auxiliary forces, to provide the food for our survival, and now much food for thought. They will not be forgotten.

Llyn Aubrey, Nickie Carlyon, Diana Ayres, Angie Butler, Melissa Hardie
The Land Army Project Team
The Hypatia Trust, Penzance
March 2006

The Women's Land Army: An Historical Review

By Mary Quick, St Ives

In 1917, three years after the outbreak of World War I, food supplies were so low that a new organisation to combat the shortage was created by Roland Pethero, then Minister of Agriculture. Hundreds of young women answered the call to serve their country in its serious need.

In June 1939, appeals were again made for young women to work on the land, and thousands of trained Women's Land Army (WLA) members were sent into employment. The WLA was part of the Ministry of Agriculture and run entirely by women for women, the Honorary Director being Lady Denham OBE, who gave her own home, Balcombe Place, as headquarters for the organisation.

Government poster published in 1917.

The WLA was well organised, and recruiting suitable girls depended upon agreement with the War Cabinet, Ministry of Labour, National Farmers' Union and National Union of Agricultural Workers, while the Agricultural Wages Board dealt with wages. Annual estimates had to be submitted to the Treasury, including training costs, uniform supplies, travelling and hostel expenses; Land Army hostels were the responsibility of the Ministry of Labour and Works.

Counties were organised separately, each county having its own Organising Secretary, Committee and Local Representative. The job of the representative was a personal and detailed one, requiring a great deal of tact. A girl who had to adjust quickly to life on the land could suffer much stress, and the poor, harassed rep had to discipline, persuade, warn and comfort each girl in her numerous troubles, feel and express relief at her contentment and happiness, and remember that Land Girls were employed by individual farmers and not by the state. At the end of the day, the rep was acting on behalf of the County Office, and it was the County Secretary who saw that all conditions of employment were met, the Land Army not being subject to military discipline.

In March 1941, Ernest Bevin, Minister of Labour, proposed the call-up of British women to assist in the war effort. Registration of 20- and 21-year-olds was announced for the following month, though pregnant women and mothers with young children were exempt. Many girls too young to be conscripted in the forces or directed to factory work voluntarily joined the WLA, although conscripts could also opt for the service. They were from all walks of life: the slums of Liverpool, Yorkshire mining towns, high-street shops and a variety of offices, all coming together with others used to wealth and privilege. At maximum strength in 1943, the Land Army numbered more than 80,000 women, all requiring billets and uniforms. The latter were usually delivered to the girls' homes.

What did you do in the war, Granny?

WE ASSOCIATE land girls with the Second World War, but the first Women's Land Army was in fact formed in 1917 when it was apparently discovered that there was only a three-week food supply left in the country.

The first WLA was a far slimmer force than the vastly more organised one that succeeded it. Its numbers never rose above 23,000. By 1943, however, 90,000 women had enrolled in a highly trained force, which, quite literally, kept a nation from starvation. The women were expected to take on all the jobs the men had done, from tractor-driving to milking, from ploughing to hedge-laying.

It was a heroic, though largely unrewarded effort. When a land girl left the WLA — it was not disbanded till 1950 as many former farm workers declined to return to the land — she received neither medal nor demob pay. It was only in 1977, after years of campaigning on the part of the British Women's Land Army Society, that the WLA was finally allowed to send a representative to the annual Festival of Remembrance at London's Albert Hall.

What every land girl did receive, and many still treasure, is a letter from the patron of the WLA, then the Queen, now the Queen Mother. It read: "Your unsparing efforts at a time when the victory of our cause depended on the utmost use of the resources of our land have earned for you the country's gratitude."

Although not particularly stylish, the uniforms could be made "smart" if worn with good posture. The full costume consisted of forest-green jersey, brown breeches, Aertex cotton shirt, heavy fawn overcoat, brown shoes for best wear, and felt slouch hats that were usually worn at a jaunty angle. Also provided were black Wellingtons, hob-nailed boots, sou'wester and oilskins as well as dungarees.

For most it was to be a rude awakening. Sent to training centres for a few weeks, the early rising and backbreaking chores, along with hard toil in all weathers, soon had the girls wondering why they had ever succumbed to the glamorous advertising posters! They were trained in all kinds of farm work. Milking by hand was still an essential skill on dairy farms, as milking machines were uncommon in remote areas including the far South West. Knowledge of dairy procedures was taught along with ploughing, planting and harvesting and other aspects of farm life.

After training, girls were despatched to all parts of the country. The South West received its allocation in addition to local girls, usually farmers' daughters already employed on district farms. In spite of the hardships, those who served with the WLA look back on the experience with nostalgia – distance lending enchantment, perhaps?

The Daily Telegraph, March 12, 1994

No weapon ever invented is more deadly than hunger; it can spike guns, destroy courage, and break the will of the most resolute peoples. The finest armies in the world, courageous enough in the face of bombs or bullets, can be reduced by it to helplessness and surrender.

This is the story of Britain's battlefield – the land; and of how 300,000 farms, strong-points in the battle against hunger, were armed, equipped and manned, so that the rich though neglected soil of these islands could be won back to fertility and help to feed and sustain a nation at war.

– From "War comes to the land," Chapter 1, *Land at War*

There are so many obvious things which get forgotten. The volunteer should always be punctual in her hours; she should not smoke about the place, especially in farm buildings; she should shut gates behind her; she should put tools back properly, so that the next person who wants them can find them; she should never leave a job half done just because she finds it difficult.

A farmer is not made in a month, and, after training, some girls are inclined to try to teach the farmer his business, often with unfortunate results. So if a volunteer has been taught a method different from the farmer's, she should always ask his permission before making the change. Farmers have no time to bother with fussy volunteers. They expect girls who have offered to do the work to carry it out without complaint.

A volunteer who enrols to "see if she likes it" is a liability, not an asset. However patriotic she may feel, she does not help her country by enrolling in the Land Army unless she is certain she can stay the course....

– From "Land Girl: A Handbook for the Women's Land Army," 1941, p. 94.

CHAPTER 1

Joining Up – and Dressing Like It!

Mary Quick writes:

Born in Wales but living in London, Betty Williams joined the Land Army in 1944 aged 18. After swearing to serve King and country she was measured for a uniform and informed that shortly she would be told where training had been arranged. This turned out to be the Duchy Farm at Stoke Climsland near Callington. Upon receiving the news, her mother called in the neighbours to view on the map this place at the ends of earth to which her daughter had been appointed! Little did they all realise that her life would be changed forever.

When the uniform arrived it was tried on, and Betty paraded up and down the high street as she was the only one in the area to have joined the service. Everybody was intrigued. This was when she got blisters for the first time from wearing heavy brogue shoes. A big farewell party was held, and Betty received "going-away" presents upon leaving home for the first time. Fortunately, at Paddington Station she met up with other Land Army recruits who were travelling to the same destination, and they quickly became friends, staying together throughout their weeks of training.

Digging for Memories

When I was 17 I joined the WLA along with two friends. When the forms came through my friends' parents would not sign for them to go, but my mother did and duly arrived my uniform. I was placed at first in Cornwall.

– Iris Woodcock, Kent

The day my parcel of clothes, rail ticket and destination instructions arrived was a real life-changing day to me. Destination Penzance. "Where the heck is Penzance?" I had to search on the map of England. Father said, "Any further and [you] would have fallen off the end." Here was I, a girl who had never been more than a cycle ride out of Leeds apart from a holiday in Bridlington once a year, going into the great unknown, and in uniform.

The uniform – I had never worn trousers before – fawn shirt, green tie, and heavy woollen sweater. With a great coat I felt like Humpty Dumpty. Father took me to train in Leeds, telling me all the way how sorry I would be to leave all the comforts of my own home. I felt this man just doesn't realize, this is my chance to get away! As my sister had also decided to join a nursing group, we both left home at the same time. We picked up girls in uniform all along the line, until four changes and 24 hours later, we arrived at Penzance.

– Micky Bowman, Penzance

I first heard about the Land Army when I was in Cardiff. I am Welsh. It was either nursing, munitions or forces. I wanted to be a nurse because previous to that I was in the Girl Guides. I used to go to the hospital to roll the bandages, but in the end my father would not allow me to go because it was a TB hospital. So I went into Cardiff town and saw the apple trees and the recruitment carts for the Land Army. I enquired, went home and told my parents and had hell. For two months I did not hear anything, then the papers came through for Penzance. My father said, "You are not going down there, my lady, it's pirates and smugglers – it's the end of England."

– Eileen 'Taff' Williams, Penzance

Ann Skewes

UNIFORMITY
2 short-sleeved shirts
1 green pullover
1 pair corduroy breeches
2 pairs socks   1 pair shoes
1 bib and brace overall
1 hat   1 pair rubber boots
1 long (very thin!)
Mackintosh
for winter

Too young to be called up and eager to "do my bit," I volunteered for war work on my 18th birthday (1944). I had taught myself aircraft spotting when 14 and passed the Marines' Recognition tests when stationed at the top of Raginnis Hill, Mousehole. At 15/16 I had done office work and switchboard at the Territorial Army Headquarters at Trereife, Newlyn, and was a junior officer in the GTC, and worked regularly with the ATC and Sea Cadets on many occasions. But when I came of age, there were no vacancies in the services for anything other than office work, so I opted for the Women's Land Army. The first farm I was sent to for training was in Devon and one of the saddest farms ever. I was familiar with several farms in West Penwith, and by comparison they were of Royal Duchy standard. The farmers were hardworking people, as all farmers are, but they were eaten up with meanness and hatred for other human beings and more especially of animals. They never spoke to me except to shout out what I had to do.
– Polly Walker, Penzance

I was born in South Wales. My first job was in the ammunitions factory near Bridgend. When the factory closed, I went to join the Forces. The only job available at the time was the Women's Land Army. This was unknown to my parents, and they weren't best pleased, but I got around them. I was sent to Penzance, Cornwall. I soon settled down, but it was tough going. Meeting so many good friends made it easier. We were a good crowd and worked all over Cornwall.
– Iris Ruberry, Porthleven

I was born at Kitts Court (where Woolworth's is now) in Penzance. I wanted to join the ATS, and went for a medical. Once we got up there to Redruth, where the signing on was, they told us that for the ATS you had to be 17-1/2 for sure. We weren't, so Mr Sampson said the best you could do is to join the Land Army, where you don't have to be a certain age. We signed our names in Penzance, and they allotted us to farms. I started off in Gulval and went to thrashing machines with two others (Gladys, Sophie and me) and an Italian and some German POWs. They gave us the hardest work, but we had some good jobs as well. I stayed in the Land Army until it finished.
– Florrie Coogan, Penzance

Washing both ourselves and our clothes was fairly primitive. There was an old bath in the dairy, with a curtain round it. Sometimes rats used to run around us and washed themselves in a bucket. We did our uniform and undies in a bucket as well.
– Betty Clark, Queensland

Top photo: Miss E.M. Goodwin, "WLA No. 124366"

Bottom photo: Jeanne Mason, in a studio portrait at Bridport, 1943.

Digging for Memories

I was brought up on a farm and decided I wanted to join the WAAFS, but my brother in the Air Force said "no way" must I join the WAAFS. So my friend and I decided to join the Land Army. Trained at Cullarian Farm, Ludgvan, under Miss Nicholls with 14 Yorkshire girls. We learnt to milk cows by hand and machine. Being Cornish I made pasties and we had midnight picnics on Marazion beach. American soldiers were stationed nearby, so we went to dances and always wore a uniform to be on the safe side. A bomb dropped in one of our fields, and I kept a piece of shrapnel for years.

– Joyce Morcomb, Newquay

I joined the Land Army on June 21, 1942. My friend and I went to the cinema, and after the film a news item came on about the Land Army. It showed a land girl picking up eggs. We thought that would suit us, so we joined. All the girls we knew in Yorkshire who had joined the WLA had stayed near home but we were sent to Cornwall. I was very homesick but we were sent to work on a big farm with 20 other Land Girls. It was very hot and I was so miserable. I couldn't understand what the Cornish folk were talking about. Anyway, I married a Cornish farmer and have been here ever since. So you can guess I managed the Cornish in the end.
– Nancy Trevennen, Goldsithney

I was working at the stationery office and felt I needed to be out doing something. The stationery office was near Oldham, Lancashire. My boyfriend was away in the forces. I was not yet 17, and I went down to the employment exchange and got the papers. My father had to sign them because I was not old enough then. My mother went spare because she wanted me not to go, but my father said, "She has made her bed, let her lie in it."
– Jeanne Bardsley, Penryn

From the April 1940 issue of The Land Girl magazine. Other issues answered such burning questions as "Should Land Girls use make-up?" Answer: "This can only be a matter for personal decision, but perhaps it is worth remembering that (a) make-up on the farm is much more conspicuous than in a town; (b) country people are much less used to make-up than town folk."

I came to Cornwall in June of 1944 and was at Stoke Climsland for a month's training on the farm, which is now the Agricultural Training College. We were all trained by a lady from Boscastle called Jane Old. My first farm was at Pendoggett. Then I went to New Mill, the other side of Penzance, and then to Carn Brea. I met my future husband while at Pendoggett. His father was crippled with arthritis and he needed help, so we got married, and on the 10th of March I will have been here on the same farm for 60 years. My eldest son is now the farmer. My husband passed on 16 years ago.
– Gwen Finnemore, Bodmin

For Kathleen Crispin (then Chilwell), signing up for the Land Army was a chance to return to Cornwall, the place of her birth. The young Kathleen travelled from Hertfordshire to the village of Ludgvan, near Penzance, for her basic four weeks of training. From there she joined a local farm and was immediately confronted with one of farming's more dramatic moments.

"The first experience I had was to help with a cow that was calving. A rope was attached to its feet and we had to gently help to pull it away," said Kathleen, who found she had an affinity with animals. "At this farm, I reared a calf, taught it to walk with a halter and took it to Lostwithiel market, where the auctioneer sold it."

She worked alongside other farmworkers with the milking, hedge-trimming, tractor-driving and dung spreading, but there were also light-hearted moments.

"One day, the men found a nest of mice and put them into my milking coat pocket only for me to put my hand in to all those wriggly things.

"We had German prisoners of war working on the farm. In their spare time, they made a garden seat and trelliswork for the farmer."

She remembers taking apples to sell at the local market and realizing that she didn't know what type they were, christened them Cornish Reds for the day, which seemed to satisfy customers.

– Chris Ferris, reporting for the Western Morning News, *1998*

Inscribed on back of photo: "To the grandest girl of all. With love, luck and best wishes for all times. Daisy."

5

Florence Phaby Lawley, formerly of Illogan, near Redruth, worked on a dairy farm near Truro

I was in a big department store, in charge of the children's department in Manchester. So decided I'd like to be Land Girl — waited, and was told I was coming down to Redruth. Didn't know where Redruth was. Mother and I had to sit and pore over an atlas to find it.
— *Jean Thomas, Helston*

At the beginning of the war my mother advised me not to sign up to anything, because more interesting jobs would materialise. She had been a VAD in the First World War. So I spent the first winter of the war helping out on the home farm at my grandfather's house in Somerset. I already knew the Bolitho family, and also Mrs Charles Williams of Trewidden, and they invited me to come down to West Cornwall. So I came to Trengwainton in March, 1940, and lived in the house. Later that summer a sort of demonstration was held at Roseworthy Barton, to show the farmers what Land Girls could do and help with. And the Bolithos wanted me very much to go because I could do most things. So I signed on to the Land Army and there I remained for 10 years, until 1950.
— *Lady Bolitho, Penzance*

I was a court dressmaker in London, making for the royalty in Knightsbridge, and made ballgowns and coming-out gowns and also for the Queen of Czechoslovakia, who was here during the war. I knew I wanted to join something and I always liked the country, so I joined the Land Army. My mother wanted me to go to Kent, but I was sent to Bodmin in Cornwall. This was odd, because before I got my posting, I had got out the map and my finger pointed to Penzance. My mother said you cannot possibly go there as it is too far away. In any event, I did not like it in Bodmin. I had two days to learn to ride a bike and then rode five miles everyday to the nearest farm (from the hostel). I put in for a transfer within a short time and got to Penzance after all.
— *Vera James, Penzance*

Joan Benney went from a London estate office to a dairy farm at Carnon Downs – and never left Cornwall

I did not know Cornwall — end of the world, really — about five of us volunteered to come down [from Lincolnshire where they were first assigned]. We arrived on the 9th of May, 1949, the day after Flora Day, picked up by a lorry and taken out to the hostel. Then the lorry picked us up every day and took us from farm to farm. After a while, when the WLA dwindled off and finished, I stayed down here and actually got married to the farmer's son. It was the last farm I worked on near Godolphin, Breage. I stayed on after and worked on the farm for quite a while, and have been a farmer's wife ever since.

— *Olive Benney, Carleen*

I was called up while living in Manchester in 1942. I had never heard of Penzance before I was sent to Cornwall. I used to be in the packing department of a factory in Manchester. When we arrived in Penzance I thought it was wonderful. Five of us were chosen to go straight to St Hilary and were billeted there. About 35 girls altogether stayed in the Old Vicarage; it was wonderful. I don't live very far from it now.

– Agnes Jilbert, St Hilary

I joined the WLA in 1944 and was one of 50 recruits travelling from the north of England to Penzance. I would never have been forgiven if my mother had thought that I hadn't been conscripted. My mother and father were rather afraid of authority and would not have doubted it if I came home and said I had been conscripted. That would be it. I never thought when the war started in 1939 and I was a schoolgirl aged 13, that in 1944 I would be called up to do some form of work to help the war effort. I realised things must be getting pretty desperate if they needed me. I went along to the recruitment office to see if I could help. At this time I was working in the clothing industry so they thought I would be good at making parachutes or making service uniforms. But I fancied a change, and had always been a tomboy, so I was offered engineering or even ATS or the nursing service. At the end of the interview, when I am sure they were beginning to despair, I said, "Could I join the Land Army?"

I left Leeds at 4 p.m. and arrived in Penzance at 4 p.m. the next day. We were met by Mr Garrett, the district manager, who divided us into two groups, and I became in charge of one group, and we walked to Ponsandane Hostel, which had been pointed out to me by a Cornish lady on the train. The other group was taken by lorry to Kenneggy Hostel.

– Micky Bowman, Penzance

I am English, born in Malta, and my family were holidaying in England in 1939. I was 13 when war broke out, and my father was recalled to Malta, and we were not allowed to return to our home there. As my mother and sister (nine years my senior) were free to live anywhere, we stayed temporarily with an aunt in Portsmouth, where I finished my schooling.

As the raids got bad my mother decided we should go to Cornwall, from where my sister got a job with the Admiralty in Bath and I went to the School of Art in Penzance until I was called up at age 18-1/2. I decided to go on the land because my mother was unwell and needed help at home as she had arranged to look after bombed babies at home (the first one stayed for life!).

I adored Cornwall. We rented a sweet home in Goldsithney and I walked to Perranuthnoe to Mr Laity's farm every morning at 6.30 to be there at 7. It was very hard work (which I wasn't used to, of course!) but so rewarding. In winter I'd leave home in the dark and my footsteps echoed in the lane as my hob-nailed boots crunched on the tarmac. No fear of "weirdos" lurking in the hedges then – until it was light the farmhands and we girls would sit in the barn round a huge table with a lantern in the middle cutting up the seed potatoes. That was the easy bit. The Cornish farm labourers were so kind to us, and kept us in fits of laughter with their stories – some pretty earthy!

– Joy Micallef, Germany

Top photo, written on the back: "To remind you of the smashing time we spent at Kenegie Hostel, Penzance. With love, from Doreen 2/12/45"

Bottom photo, written on the front: "To a dear friend I'll never forget. Love, Gladys." On the back: "Do I really look as daft as this."

WOMEN'S LAND ARMY SONG

Back to the land, we must all lend a hand,
To the farms and the fields we must go.
There's a job to be done,
Though we can't fire a gun,
We can still do our bit with the hoe...
Back to the land, with its clay and its sand,
Its granite and gravel and grit,
You grow barley and wheat
And potatoes to eat
To make sure that the nation keeps fit...
We will tell you once more
You can help win the war
If you come with us – back to the land.

CHAPTER 2

Going There – Being Here

Name...Miss Leonora Alison Simpson.

No....36293.

You are now a member of the Women's Land Army. You are pledged to hold yourself available for service on the land for the period of the war. You have promised to abide by the conditions of training and employment of the Women's Land Army; its good name is in your hands. You have made the home fields your battlefield. Your country relies on your loyalty and welcomes your help.

Signed...C. Denman...   Honorary Director

Signed...Mary Williams...   Chairman Committee

Date.... 10th October, 1940.....

I realise the national importance of the work which I have undertaken and I will serve well and faithfully.

Signed... Leonora A. Simpson.

I always remember I was not used to the accent and said to my mum, "I think all the men down here are called Harry." I realised after a while it was a Cornish way of talking and people were saying, "All right, ar' ee?"
– *Peggy Godding, Helston*

Top photo: Lower Sticker Farm, St Austell, 1949-50

Left: Land Girls from Ponsandane, Kenneggy and Poltair

Digging for Memories

From my hometown of Bromley in Kent, I applied to join the Land Army in 1943, and was accepted immediately. A week later, a letter informed that I would be located in the West Country, and my sister, joining at the same time, was being sent to Northampton.

When we first arrived at Penzance station, it was foggy, grey and misty. My first thought was "Why am I here?" It seemed quite a miserable place. The bleakness made me homesick for the lush verdant grass and swaying trees of Kent. But we were made so welcome by Mr Ben and Beatrice, the lady in charge of us, that my worries and misgivings went away. I felt excited. I was embarking on an adventure, and I was determined to enjoy it.

– *Ellen Prowse, Sennen*

Elevenses during threshing at Cullarian Farm, St Erth (photo courtesy of Betty Clark)

My joy knew no bounds. I thought: this is paradise, I shall never leave this place. When I arrived at the station, the girls, all in uniform, piled off to be met by a Mr Garrett, who was in charge. There were about 50 of us. Half of the luggage had to go to Ponsandane Hostel and the other half to Kenegie.

– *Micky Bowman, Penzance*

I came from Wigan, when I was 18. The reason I joined the Land Army was that I was working in a sewing factory and was making uniforms. We heard that some of us would be sent to work in ammunitions, and my friend and I didn't like the idea of that – girls walking around town with yellow faces were in ammunitions – so we went straightaway and joined the Land Army. My father was in the Navy, one uncle was in the Air Force, another in the Army, so I thought Land Army was for me. It took us 12 hours to come down on the steam train to Cornwall, standing most of the way.

– *Alice Talling, Llanteglos by Fowey*

Cornishman July 12th, 1939, page 6

The Women's Land Army in Cornwall

RECRUITS URGENTLY NEEDED

We have received the following report on the progress of the Women's Land Army in Cornwall:

The committee is now complete, but helpers with organisation [-al skills] will be welcomed, particularly those who had experience in the last war.

Chairman, Mrs. E H W Bolitho; organising secretary, Mrs Pollard, St Mawes; propaganda recruiting officer, Miss Calmady-Hamlyn; Miss Collett (Women's Farm and Garden Association representative); Mrs A Martin, Mrs Favell (St Ives West), Miss R Cruddas (Bodmin), Miss W [...] (North and East Cornwall), Miss I. Dorrie[...] (Falmouth and Penryn). Mrs Ward (C[...] Redruth).

Volunteers are coming in well and we have had a gratifying response from Cornish farmers to our appeal to take a girl for a fortnight's free training with board and lodging. We are proud to say that these farmers have not demanded the payment of 15s a week suggested by the Ministry, which would have to be paid by the trainees themselves since no grant is being made to help with training. But these generous and public-spirited farmers have offered board and lodging free during the training, which is a gesture that the Ministry should deeply [appre]ciate. It reflects credit on the county.

The bulk of our volunteers are, however, women [wit]h practical experience of farming and most of them [wi]ll not need peace-time training. This disposes of the [th]eory that Cornish farmers' wives and daughters would [n]ot support the Land Army but choose jobs that would take them away from the land in war-time, leaving town girls to do the business of food production. The farmers' wives and daughters are our most staunch supporters, and if the disaster of war should overtake us we shall find a magnificent body of Cornishwomen prepared to cultivate the soil of Cornwall and maintain our food supplies.

Further information gladly supplied by the organizing secretary, Mrs Pollard, The Ropewalk, St Mawes.

Cornishman June 26th, 1941

"BETTER TO BUILD UP THAN DESTROY"

MEETING OF LAND ARMY GIRLS

"Don't the cows and other animal noises keep you awake at nights?" I asked.

"Oh, dear me, no; they only send me to sleep," said a young Lancashire lassie, Betty Barrow of Manchester, when I spoke to her up at the farm adjoining the house at Trengwainton (residence of the Lord-Lieutenant of Cornwall, Lieut.-Colonel E H W Bolitho, and Mrs Bolitho) on Tuesday evening.

Betty was one of the forty-two girls from all parts of the British Isles, who have come to these idyllic surroundings, and who, as a member of the Women's Land Army, is enjoying life to the uttermost.

She came from Manchester, said this young fair-haired girl, and she was a machinist in a cotton factory when she volunteered for the Women's Land Army.

"And I love Cornwall," added Betty, "though, of course, I love Lancashire more, because, you see, I coom from there." (As if she needed to tell me that, with her gorgeous Northcountry brogue.)

A Jolly, Healthy Crowd

Let it not be thought that I had gone to Trengwainton [now National Trust] just to see what the girls of the Women's Land Army looked like! Far from it.

Indeed, I approached the door of their habitation with some trepidation! Within, I could hear the sounds of laughter and merriment! I opened the door—somewhat sheepishly—to find myself in the midst of a bevy of rosy-cheeked, smiling, typically British girls.

Their very looks—exuding health and well-being—were a tribute to their short time with the Women's Land Army.

These girls are going to be a very real help to the farmers: nay, they are that already.

Those at Trengwainton form the nucleus of one of the first two hostels in Cornwall—the other, at Gulval, was opened simultaneously about a fortnight ago.

They have come to help in lifting the potato crop, after which, should there be no seasonal work about at which they can be utilised, they will go through their course of training, and will then be posted to various farms throughout the country.

An Enthusiastic Meeting

In point of fact, I went to hear the girls addressed by Mr Lionel Rogers, chairman of the Cornwall War Agriculture Committee. The chair was taken by Mrs Charles Williams, president of the Women's Land Army in Cornwall, others present being Mrs Lionel Rogers, Mr J Wilson (executive officer of the Cornwall War Agriculture Committee), Mrs Clifford Smith (secretary of the Women's Land Army in Cornwall), Mrs E H W Bolitho and Mrs Molesworth St Aubyn (members of the Committee), and Mrs Curtis (welfare superintendent), who sees to the girls' comfort.

In a brief speech, Mr Lionel Rogers under the aegis of whose Committee these girls have been brought to the West Cornwall district to assist in lifting the potato crop, said the object of his Committee was to get the utmost from every field in the country.

After describing the system under which the Cornwall War Agricultural Committee worked, and dealt with the 14,000 farmers in Cornwall, Mr Rogers went on: "You are helping your country by producing as much food as possible, so that we shall not be starved out."

He referred to the shipping losses, and how production at home would save valuable space in vessels coming to this country.

Expressing his pleasure at the good work the girls were doing, Mr Rogers said: "Your work is of great importance. Nearly everyone is either making or using weapons of destruction. You are using your skill and work to feed people and keep them alive. It is better to build up than to destroy."

Mr Lionel Rogers went on to refer to the conservatism of farmers who were at first prejudiced against the Women's Land Army, but he added, "Everywhere you girls have gone, farmers have been converted."

Mr Wilson referred to the value of the work of the girls in the absence of the men, whose promised transfer from the Army had not materialised.

Proposing a vote of thanks to the speakers, Doris Casley, especially praised the work of Mrs Charles Williams and her helpers. Doris is a dark-haired girl from Devon. Country-bred,

she is no stranger to the life she is now leading, but she said that she loved it in the Women's Land Army—and she certainly looked as if she meant it.

So, too, did little Margaret Snelling also hailing from Devon. She was typical of every girl there with her smiling face and cheery manner. No wonder Mrs Bolitho said that she liked to hear them singing at nights – these lasses just couldn't help singing.

Incidentally, besides Devon, Cornwall and Lancashire, there were girls from Sussex, Kent, Essex, London and Somerset, not forgetting one Scottie.

Mrs Curtis was loudly applauded – she is a most popular "mother" to the girls; Colonel and Mrs Bolitho were thanked for enabling the hostel to be used, to which Mrs Bolitho said that the credit for all the work belonged, not to her, but to Mrs Williams and Mrs St Aubyn.

So this happy, jolly, care-free meeting was over. Only two conclusions can be drawn – no girl will regret her choice if she joins the Women's Land Army, and surely no farmer will regret giving the girls the chance to take the places of men, as they are only too eager to, and have already done so successfully.

So they trooped off to the fields to wait a mythical photographer (at least, he had not turned up when I left). I hope he came . . .

NWW

Written on back of top photo: "To Taff, Love & best wishes, Sylvia. 1945"

Middle: "Friends forever, Lots of love, Taff"

Above: "Remember us always. Taff. WLA"

Left: Sea View, Sennen (collection of Ellen Ash Prowse)

I joined the Land Army in 1941 and was sent to Carbis Bay to the family Beckerleg. I was the first Land Girl they had and I lived with the family. It was a mixed farm, mostly dairy as there were four milk rounds and I was allotted one of the rounds.

As time went on three more girls were taken on. Apart from milking by hand with other employees 45 Guernsey shorthorns, I did all the other chores – bunching anemones, picking up potatoes, cutting cabbage and broccoli. A total of nine employees, plus the owners, were kept in full-time employment.

– *Fay Beckerleg, St Ives*

I started at a farm at Falmouth but didn't like it, so I was transferred to Creens Farm, Ladock, where I spent most of my working time in the Land Army.

I arrived there on a very wet afternoon after cycling up from Probus Halt (with the directions "go up the road till you have gone two miles then turn left"). Anyway, I found it, and Granfer was out in the cart shed with the youngest member of the family, Clive, 2-1/2 years old, and I asked, "Is this Creens Farm, please?" It seems Granfer didn't know who I was, and replied, "What the bloody hell are you talking about?" I wondered what I had come to, but we had a lot of laughs about it when he came in and found the Land Maid was here. I've so many memories. I met my husband that first day, when he came in late from the fields, and we had 58 years together.

– *Joan Goodman, St Austell*

Photo courtesy of Agnes Jilbert.

Coming from London, I trained at the Duchy of Cornwall Farm at Stoke-Climsland, after joining up in 1944 – I remember the Royal Standard Flag flying from the lodge in honour of Princess Margaret's birthday 21st August. My first farm was at Trebor Cross Roads, where Goonhilly Satellite Station now stands, helping out a farmer who was in hospital. It was busy, being harvest time. We had a half-day off once a week. I cycled into Helston on my half days passing big Laing lorries busy all day long building the now Culdrose Naval Air Base Station. My second and final farm was Trescowe. There we were, three Land Girls plus four local farm hands. Helping out were three Italian POWs followed by three German POWs. They travelled in lorries from the Clowance lodges in Praze.

Great celebrations on 8th May 1945, VE Day, as Newtown was only about six miles from Helston, and, of course, it was Flora Day. I met my husband in Trescowe, because he worked as an agricultural mechanic repairing tractors and combine harvesters. After we married in 1948, he worked Marazion way putting in milking machines as that entailed a lot of work. I have stayed here ever since.

– *Peggy Godding, Helston*

My memories of Cornwall and the Land Army are mixed. Billeted in Gulval, I took a bus to Hayle daily; later billeted in Truro. Often we walked between farms in Helston, and eventually remained at Mr McClaren's. I am still in touch with the children of two Helston farmers. On one farm in Penryn, we did not get on with the farmer as we went to the pictures on Sunday! I also remember a farmer who treated Italian prisoners of war better than Land Girls, and a farmer who left dead animals to rot in the field. Standing all the way from Truro to Paddington is another memory. Good memories include being given fresh eggs to take home to my mother when I had to leave. I regret not having remained in Cornwall after the war.

– Ivy Gordon, London

Inset from *Milking practice with artificial udders* 1940, by Evelyn Dunbar (Imperial War Museum, London)

I arrived in Cornwall from Ruislip, Middlesex, January 1940 to start training at Tregarthen's farm, Collurian, Ludgvan. I vividly remember arriving cold and hungry after the long train journey and being shown my living quarters – a converted hen house. A strange and different life had begun. After six weeks I was transferred to Fowey to work on a large mixed farm. I loved the life and was very happy there except for the fact that the farmer's wife thought that this 18-year-old girl might be a threat to her, where her husband (at least 60 years old) was concerned. I asked for a transfer and was sent to a large mixed farm near St Columb Minor. Again I was very happy and gained so much experience. I was encouraged to take exams in husbandry and animal welfare, and now I still see the farmer's daughter with whom I worked.

– Irene Karkeek, Newquay

From the autumn of 1941 I worked around Cornwall, at Millpool, Cardinham, then in and around Bodmin, before transferring to a market garden in Penzance. After the threshing season I was sent to Truro and worked on various farms. At the end of that assignment I went on to Wiltshire to join my younger sister there. I was sorry to leave Cornwall. Lovely county.

– Phyllis Stern, Hertfordshire

TO ALL LAND GIRLS

FROM AN ADMIRER OF THEIR WORK.

I saw a Land Girl working
    Alone in an open field.
Her hard, once elegant, hands
    A stalwart hoe did wield.
Her back was bent as she slew the weeds
    That spoiled the potatoes' growth;
She never wilted, she never paused,
    She had taken her silent oath.

At last the day was nearly done,
    The sun was sinking low;
She gathered up her jacket
    Then slowly cleaned her hoe.
She passed the chair where I sat
    (I am feeble in body and sight).
She smiled at me as she said:
    "Been hot to-day. Good-night."

We hear the valiant deeds of our men in
    "furrin parts,"
Deeds which bring the tears to our eyes, a
    glow of pride to our hearts –
But when the war is over and peace at last
    restored,
I shall always remember the Land Girl, who
    made her hoe her sword.

CHAPTER 3

Housing and Home

The living arrangements for Land Army girls varied in the extreme. Some never left home but worked on neighbouring farms. Some left homes in the north to find new and often lasting homes in the South West. Most, however, were trained in groups, staying at training centres from up to six weeks, and then being billeted in hostels around the county, or individually with the farming families requesting their help.

As the news cuttings indicate, requests were put in by farmers for one or more helpers, and the local committee matched up these requests with the Land Army girls willing and capable of taking the challenge. Not every match was ideal, and transfers were available if the assignment was unworkable. Religious intolerance and difficult attitudes to women occasionally marred the "project." Some of the living conditions were basic, even grim and unspeakably awful on individual farms. But overall, the need to pull together – while making some strange partnerships – made everyone as cooperative as possible in generally tough times.

THE LAND GIRLS: All rookies together away from home

Great friendship forged at hostel

A new film called The Land Girls, which was filmed in the Westcountry, opens later this year. Since we previewed the movie, readers have been keen to tell us what it was really like in the Women's Land Army. **DAVID GREEN** talks to three more land girls

● **STILL IN TOUCH:** Mary Keverne, Hannah Pascoe and Iris Ruberry pictured in Helston in 1945, above, and in 1998, below 18/3/98,

THREE teenage Land Girls sent to West Cornwall, hundreds of miles from their homes, in 1945 are still great friends who get together regularly to chat about the old times.

Hannah Pascoe, Mary Keverne and Iris Ruberry were among 20 girls living in a large house which was requisitioned for them in Lady Street, Helston.

They have fond memories of those days though Hannah admitted: "I don't suppose it was much fun cutting broccoli in the freezing mornings but you only remember the good times and there were plenty of those."

Hannah was from Oldham in Lancashire and the other two from Wales but none went home again because they all fell in love and married local men.

They used to work in gangs on local farms. "We used to do any farmwork that the farmers needed doing," explained Hannah.

"We all volunteered to be Land Girls and I was originally sent to Hayle for a month before being moved to Helston. There were two wardens at the house where we lived but we still managed to enjoy ourselves."

Hannah, a widow, lives at Kingsley Way, Helston. She has a son, Martin, who also lives in Helston and a grandson, Gavin.

She and Mary have helped run Helston Darby and Joan Club for the past 10 years and they regularly see Iris, who has recently moved to Porthleven.

Mary remembers: "We worked very long hours, seven days a week but we loved it. We were all rookies together. We were away from home and in our teens and the companionship was beautiful.

"I was in the Land Army in Wales before I came to Cornwall. I must have liked it because I'm still here."

She and her husband, Billy, a retired blacksmith, live at Osborne Parc, Helston. They have a daughter, Loretta, who farms at Quethiock, near Liskeard, and two grandchildren.

Hannah added that the ex-Land Girls who were based in Helston still hold reunions to exchange news of families and events.

"As time goes by our numbers are getting less but still about a dozen of us get together to reminisce about old times."

The Western Morning News, March 18, 1998

Mary Quick writes:

Headquarters at Stoke Climsland was the lovely old manor house, and the girls were welcomed by the matron, Miss Old, who showed them to their rooms, each containing six bunks. After unpacking, a meal was served and then they lined up for an inspection by the matron, hands held out. Miss Old passed down the line saying "Cut, cut, cut" to those with long nails. A few girls protested, but she told them, "Right, tomorrow at 6:30 in the morning you will know why I want short nails." To some girls this was puzzling, as they perhaps had never seen a cow?

Previous to joining the Land Army in 1942, I was in charge of my uncle's dairy business. Being also a farmer's daughter, I was sent to work on a farm in Germoe, so was able to home on my weekend off. I would have preferred to live on the farm, but this was not possible, and my experience of lodgings was pretty grim. I had to share a bed. Thankfully the other girl was very clean. No hot water, no flush toilet. We had to beg water to wash and go across the yard to the toilet. I think perhaps a hostel would have been a happier place.
– *Jean Trevaskis, Helston*

I remember the homesickness to start with. I came from West Bromwich and I was sent to Hayle, where I was billeted at the Penmare Hostel, which became the Penmare Hotel, and now is no more. We were eight to a room. I was 278 miles from home, the first time ever away. After the first couple of weeks I could start to eat again. I was 19. I enjoyed the apple pies and the cream we used to pinch out of the curd from the churns.
– *Joyce Tooth, Newquay*

Bedroom was a barn!

We arrived from Lancashire at St Erth Station in the middle of the afternoon and a taxi was waiting to take us to the training centre. The visions I had in my mind about this place were anything but what we found on arriving.

First, it was a very misty day. We could see nothing but the hedgerows. It was a dismal, miserable afternoon. Our bedroom was a barn, very primitive washing facilities. And the loo – I used to whip in and out of that as quickly as possible! It was an earthen closet, a wooden seat with a hole but no bucket. Didn't it let the draught in! Some mischievous imp used to wait until one of us sat on the throne and then would stick a stinging nettle up the hole from outside.

– *Betty Nicholls,*
from A Blackley Girl in Cornwall

Timber Corps members with other Land Girls in Bath, in 1945, to collect long-service badges from HRH Princess Elizabeth (photo courtesy of Vera Lloyd)

Ponsandane
We were all assigned little bunk beds. I had never mixed with girls, lovely girls from all over the place. We were a nice mixed lot. As far as I was concerned it was like a nice little hotel.
– *Micky Bowman, Penzance*

Trevelloe House, Lamorna

I was not a Land Girl! However, my aunt, Betty Mulholland, was. We do not know where, but she was billeted somewhere in the far south west of Cornwall. My husband and I bought Trevelloe House in Lamorna two years ago. When I was finding out a little of the house's history, I came across some old Ministry of Defence Maps of the area. It then transpired that this house had been used by the Land Girls during the war. Unfortunately, my aunt has passed away now, but I often wonder if maybe she was billeted at Trevelloe House during her time in Cornwall? (She later married and emigrated to Australia.) We'd be delighted to hear of any Land Girls who stayed at the House. If any are able or close enough to visit it again, a little re-union could be organised.

– *Debra Neave, Lamorna*

Peter Wood recalls:

I was living at Redhouse on the Trevelloe Estate between Lamorna and Sheffield during the war years. My memory is that there was a group of Land Girls working in a field near Redhouse, when I must have been 3 or 4 years old. Their bags were placed near a cart and I found a packet of cigarettes. I had never seen cigarettes before and was busy taking them to bits when I was discovered. It must have been very annoying for the owner of the fags.

Cornishman March 4th, 1942

Penzance National Record

New Hostel for Land Girls Handed Over

The Powers That Be said that a Land Army hostel which has been erected at Ponsandane should be finished by midday on March lst. And it was done.

It was completed in five weeks and three days. This beat the standard time by well over three weeks, and created a new national record for war construction work.

And the reason for all this haste? It is due to the greatly-increased food production drive by farmers in this area. Over 3,000 acres of extra food crops have been put down in the Penzance district alone, and the immediate service of 150 land girls is required. Some of these girls will be billeted in the town. Fifty of them will live at the hostel, which will be staged by the YWCA.

At midday on Sunday the building was formally handed over to Mr S H Eva who accepted it on behalf of the County War Agricultural Committee.

The hostel, which is a single-storey building, consists of a welfare and staff block, ablutions block, dormitory block, laundry and drying rooms. The dining and recreation room is 50 ft by 20 ft and the dormitory 120 ft by 16 ft, containing 50 double-tier bunks. Lighting and cooking is by gas, and there are also solid fuel cookers and heating stoves.

The architect said that the record finish had only been possible by the complete and whole-hearted co-operation from all concerned, including the Penzance Gas Company. There had been from 40 to 75 men engaged on the contract, working overtime from the beginning.

Elizabeth Sparrow, Paul, writes:

I had been told that [Land Girls] were billeted in Trevelloe House . . . I was surprised in 2002 to have a visit from Joan Reilly, who said that she had been a Land Girl and that some of them were billeted in the house in 1947. She recognized the bedroom where they slept.

Poltair, near Penzance

I arrived at Penzance station and went in a cattle lorry to Poltair. It was a formidable building. I thought, "Oh dear, what have we come to." Mostly we were Londoners. Matron was in charge: 20 in bottom and 20 in the top, out of the 40 of us who got off the train. First experiences, first day or two looking at the other girls, finding out what they were like, would they like me, because all different accents and some looked cross but they had good hearts. At this hostel for a month with no work to do so just walked along the Prom looking for Yanks – dare I say, everybody else did.

– *Pat Peters, Helston*

And another Kenneggy:

I was a shorthand typist and working in Oxford Street, London. I went home one day and told my parents I had joined the Land Army. I told the recruiters I didn't mind anywhere from John O'Groats to Lands End, and I was very, very lucky I was sent down to a place called Kenneggy Farm – on the turning off right by the Coach and Horses, and I was there for a good many years. Only that one job, did not move around.

We worked hard, but the Thomases (now both dead) were very kind. We were very fortunate. It was Rosudgeon, which is not far from here where I now live.

– *Mary Pightling, Helston*

Inscription on photo above reads, "Truck Drivers W.L.A. 4/5/46."

Kenegie

The farmer and his wife, daughter and sons lived at a small place called Gulval about two miles up hill from Penzance. We lived in what had been a manor house, it was called Kenegie. It was stripped of all the furniture, we had rows of bunk beds, and there was a long, tree-lined drive up to the house. The garden had huge magnolia trees, and we had a wonderful view of St Michael's Mount.

– *Marjorie Overton-Larty, Saffron Walden*

Ladock, near Truro

In Ladock we had a large house – 52 rooms – and had prisoners of war there. Also, soldiers in tents in the fields.

– *Doreen Yelland, Truro*

List of hostels and camps in Cornwall referred to by the Land Girls:

GULVAL
Kenegie
Kenneggy (now a holiday park and hotel)

HAYLE
Penmare Hostel (now gone)

LADOCK

LAMORNA
Trevelloe House

LISKEARD
Pencubid

LOOE
Trelawn

LUDGVAN
Cullarian (Tregarthen Farm)

PENZANCE
Poltair (now a hospital)
Ponsandane (now a rest home)

SENNEN
Sea View

ST ANTHONY
Place House Holiday Camp

ST COLUMB MAJOR
The Old Rectory

ST HILARY
The Vicarage

TRURO
Truro Vean Holiday Camp

STOKE CLIMSLAND
Training Centre

Kathleen Gillbard was first assigned to Gulval, later to St Ive, between Liskeard and Callington

THE GOLDEN GIRLS

By David Prowse

They always said farmers were
    born and not made,
From fathers to sons was
    tradition conveyed.
It wasn't for learning from
    blackboard and chalk.
But something you breathed from
    the day you could walk.

Oh, a stranger could visit and
    play for a while.
He could join in the harvest and
    leave with a smile,
But his heart still belonged to the
    bustle and smoke,
Not the day-to-day grind of the
    countryman's yoke.

Then the Land Army came and
    the diehards turned green
At this giggling confection from
    Stepney and Cheam,
'The world has gone mad,' was
    the whispered critique,
'They'll be home with their
    mothers in less than a week.'

But the china-doll species they
    had in their minds
Would bear no relation to this
    urban kind;
They hadn't come calling from
    tea at the Ritz
But the bombs and the blood of
    the Luftwaffe blitz.

There was much that was lacking
    and much to be learned,
But they'd not be deflected or
    easily turned;
Just as fathers were fighting with
    bayonets and guns,
They, too, were prepared for the
    battles to come.

So the infinite mysteries of
    pastoral lore
Were embraced with the passion
    of soldiers at war,
With pikes and with shovels as
    banners and shields,
They joined with the yeomen and
    marched to the fields.

And they learned how to harvest
    potatoes and hay,
How to shuck up the corn-
    sheaves and milk twice a day,
How to cope with the backache,
    the heat and the chill,
How to hoe, how to harrow, to
    plant and to till.

And they learned about horses
    and heifers and cows
And binders and reapers and
    shufflers and ploughs,
And for many, that insight was
    all they would need
For the city's attractions to fade
    and recede.

They came with so little bar stout,
    willing hearts
To an alien culture of horses and
    carts,
They had no traditions with
    which to connect
But they rolled up their sleeves
    for a nation's respect.

When they write about wartime
    and how we survived,
There's many a victory
    conviction contrived
And many among us with reason
    to say,
'God bless the girls of the WLA.'

– David Prowse's poems have been read on BBC Radio Cornwall.

CHAPTER 4

Down to Earth: The Work

Claire Leith's story is a shining example of the peripatetic, adapting nature of a Land Girl, her work, and more often than not, the resulting satisfaction and happiness. That is not to say there were not really bad times, and experiences that took grit and determination to get through. Amongst Land Girls, the traffic was two-way, with many coming to Cornwall for the first time, and Cornish girls travelling away to other counties.

I was originally from Cape Cornwall, born at Porthledden House on the hill. I always wanted to work on a farm and used to go to Madron to work on the land on a Wednesday. Everybody was joining up so I said I wanted to go into the Land Army. My parents made sure I could hoe a field before I went. Then my aunt came down the following June and she said, "Come back to Sussex with me," and I went up there and did my training in Sussex. I was very bad at dairy work as I could not get the milk out of the cow.

I was sent to Lincolnshire to the forest. It was exciting because I had a nice landlord and landlady and I was cosseted. I had never washed in a basin before or had a copper put on to do a bath. The toilet was down the bottom of the garden. But they were lovely warm, loving people, I liked being in the open. Worked in the forest for about six months I suppose. In the forest we took trees down, saplings that needed to come down, coppicing layering. A friend and I were sent on

In Hertfordshire, similar stories were reported:

One Friday afternoon, late in 1943, I left a warm and comfortable office job in the heart of London and reported on the following Monday morning at 5 a.m. to a cold, draughty cowshed, was handed a brush and bucket and told to wash 15 cows. My first introduction to the back end of any animal!

Soon learned to milk, clean out cowsheds, pigsties, sweep yards, cut beet and kale, harness horses, build haystacks and drive a tractor. But not before in the first month having the palms of my hands and between my fingers one mass of blisters!

– Sheila Ellis, St Austell

Left: Joan Guntrip. Above: Frances Cross. Lower Sticker Farm, St Austell, 1949-50.

special journeys to pick up acorns because they wanted to save them to re-make a forest. Later I went to work in a big garden in Lincolnshire. They sent vegetables to market and I was there for some time and was loaned out to help with the harvest.

Out of the blue came the message that down in Surrey there was this farm that was used to train young men, in peace time, to work in the dairy. So down I went. Started at five in the morning, winter and summer, milked at three o'clock worked very hard. Happy there! I don't like regimentation very much and in a way Land Army was not like that.

– Claire Leith, Truro

In Essex, it was testing:
Always trying to prove that, if not as strong as the men, at least as keen to do our best. I can remember one occasion when cheered on by my fellow girls and several of the men I carried a "quarter" (a *very* large sack) of wheat (the heaviest grain) from the back of a wagon to the chute on my back. It was a one-off, and it was crazy – but I did it!

The fact that I have suffered with back pain all my life is not surprising! But what mainly sticks with me now is that I do not really care about the weather. I'd *hate* to live in a dry country. As long as I'm warm – no matter about getting a little wet. I never use an umbrella!

– Ann Foreman, Hayle

Lois Pulford writes from Ross on Wye in Herefordshire:

Cornish farms in the 1940's were primitive, to say the least, and even the Women's Land Army training centre had no 'mod cons' though the cows lived in comparative luxury.

During the month of training about two dozen girls lived in a large converted chicken-house or a stable-loft, and slept in two-tier bunks (mostly flea-ridden). We cleaned our teeth at a tap in the outer wall of the pigsty, and carried water to wash into a couple of china bowls in the sleeping quarters.

As I could already hand-milk the cows I was somewhat favoured, but had to learn a complicated milkround at weekends, when the usual girl was off-duty.

Fortunately, I was there in August, but in winter it must have been deadly. We spent hours in the Harvest fields high on the backbone of West Cornwall, from which we could see the sea on both the north and south coasts.

One farm to which I was posted was run by an elderly non-conformist farmer who, on Sundays, only milked a cow or two before going in for breakfast prior to chapel. By the time I got in for my own breakfast he had a mirror propped up against the milk jug, and was shaving at the breakfast table.

Eventually I got to a farm in my father's parish, and although it was still four miles from home, I could cycle back and forth in my scarce free time. I must say that a featherbed was cosy at night (I hadn't met one before – or since), but one went to bed by candlelight, and Aladdin and Tilley lamps were the order downstairs and outside. There was a pump outside the back door, and a galvanized bowl on a chair, where everyone washed before meals, and the water only got changed when it was muddy enough!

Three or four of us usually did the milking by hand, and the farmer's sons, who had very good voices, sang hymns or the latest wartime songs while doing it.

I was given the use of an ancient horse and cart for the cleaning out of cow sheds, carting manure and fetching loads of mangolds from the fields, and once I got wedged between the stone gatepost and the shafts of the cart, which had skidded on a sharp incline. How I got free was a miracle as it was a mile from the house. Another time, after a considerable fall of snow, when taking a load to a far field, the horse's hooves kept picking up layers of snow till he could hardly walk. Mercifully, I had an old pocket knife with me, and every few yards had to stop, pick up each hoof in turn, and lever off the solid snow.

Harvest crops at that time and place consisted of wheat and "dredge-corn," a mixture of oats and barley which was ground for cattle feed after thrashing. No combine harvesters in those days, though there was a reaper and binder which chucked out the sheaves, and we then had to 'shock' them (the Cornish term for stooks) till they were dry enough to carry and build into ricks. The thrasher came by appointment, and all hands had to help. It was a filthy, dusty job, and the barley tine worked their way into all our clothes and hair.

Food on the farm was no great problem, though monotonous, as milk, cream and butter galore were available. A pig was killed at Christmas and eggs were plentiful, but although fields of cauliflowers were grown we seldom ate one – instead, every day we had mashed swede for lunch, and even when they were out of season a few were kept under the black currant bushes, so as not to break the cycle. Rice pudding was every day too, and the weekly Cornish pasty was so huge that

WOMEN'S LAND ARMY PROFICIENCY CERTIFICATE.

THIS IS TO CERTIFY THAT

Miss Ellen Ash.   W.L.A. No. 109737

HAS BEEN AWARDED A PROFICIENCY BADGE

IN Milking and Dairy Work.

Date August 1944.   Signed G. Denman.
on behalf of the Women's Land Army.

it overlapped a full-size dinner plate, though after all the outdoor labour it never seemed too much.

After such a lifestyle, imagine my panic at being thrust into a London West End rectory to help their severely handicapped teenage daughter, but that's another story…

Summer and winter and seed time and harvest,
Sun, moon and stars in their courses above,
Join with all nature in manifold witness
To Thy great faithfulness, mercy and love.

From Somerset to Cornwall:
I was in the Land Army from 1940-50 and spent the whole of that time at Trengwainton near Penzance. I actually got my 10-year badge. Very few got that because it was disbanded shortly after that.

From early 1943 I was in charge of the farm, which was a mixed farm growing broccoli, sugar beet, oats, barley, with a dairy herd of 30 or so cows and some pigs. I could plough, sow, reap and mow, build a rick and thatch it and did thrashing . . . all those sort of things. There was a tractor, a standard Fordson, but most of the work was done by horses.

We trained new recruits to the Land Army in bunches of eight or 10 for one month before they went out on to the other farms. They came from all sorts of places, mostly big towns with very little, if any, idea of what farming was all about, but they nearly all stuck it out and went on to do sterling work. Farming was very labour intensive in those days, and they certainly contributed a good deal. The girls did a lot of heavy work, and lighter work, poultry and picking potatoes, planting hoeing and looking after the livestock. Thoroughly enjoyed it and stayed in farming all my life.
– *Lady Desiree Bolitho, Penzance*

Joy Mundy (Helston) spent most of the war period (1942-45) in Worcester in mixed farming, but in 1945 she managed to get a transfer to a coastal farm at Predannack:
My mother was Mullion-born, and in 1945

my parents moved to Cornwall, where my father was a pharmacist. I transferred to a much smaller farm than I was used to, with few cattle and a milking herd. Also broccoli, cabbage, grain, hay and ploughing work. The farm was close to an airfield but there was no military contact during the working day. Sadly I was invalided out in autumn of that year with mastitis.

I first became interested when I was 20 years old, and got called up at Newlyn East. I went to train at Cullarian near Ludgvan for a month. I seemed to be on the milk round all the time. I was called "Tip and Run," but got sent to Trengwainton and stayed there for four years doing dairy work, milking, and mostly worked with Lady Bolitho. She said women did lighter work but she did her fair share of the heavy work. I have seen her carry 2cwt of manure up steps when the men would not unload them. She used to go out and do the ploughing.
– *Violet Stevens, Marazion*

Having spent one year of bombing in London, I was allowed to leave my office job and join the Land Army. What a delight to be sent to Cornwall. I trained with 12 other girls with Dora Nicholas at Collurian (White Cross) and Walter Tregarthen. We slept in a barn and Dora called us "Twits in the Twittery." I guess that summed us up!

It was fun but tough, milking cows by hand, spreading muck, planting potatoes.

At the end of the month we went our separate ways – me to Cury (Skewes Farm). My farmer was great and put up with my mistakes, e.g., upsetting all the milk churns, slicing the cabbage tops when hoeing – pulling out hay bales and rick collapsing – and to top it all I was chased by the bull.

In 1944 I got married and lived in St Ives. My wedding reception for 31 guests (Curnows Café) cost £7.14s.8p including cigs and lemonade.

– *Peggy White, St Ives*

I was working in a hatchery, we put all the eggs into the incubator and after 18 days took them out and checked them to see if they were fertile or not and then they'd go into a big incubator, and after two or three days we had all these trays full of chicks. Then they went into another place and were sexed and packed and sent off to wherever they were going. During this time of year [we were] sent up and down the county doing what they called blood testing the flocks that we were going to get the eggs from. That could be very difficult because in November time it was wet muddy fields. There were poultry, roosters and everything. We did testing to see if they were a good stock. I was at the hatchery all the time until I got married. I married the local chap who picked up the milk everyday and was a Land Girl when I married. I have lived here ever since and gone back only for holidays to Manchester. The only job I insisted I would never do was milk the cows.
Cows' houses were filthy.
– *Jean Thomas, Helston*

Photo courtesy of the Cornwall Centre,
Alma Place, Redruth, Cornwall

We were told that we would be working for the "War Agg," which meant that we would be working for any farmer needing extra help, for a day or a week, depending on the job in hand. I worked on many farms for about three months, and then I became a driver (trained by the Land Army) and so began a very interesting and varied part of my two-year stay in Cornwall. I had joined the Land Army because a friend of mine had joined up. She had not been in very long when she sent a photograph showing her with about a dozen rats in each hand, and she thought she would like to go into the pest extermination department. I suddenly realised there were all sorts of departments. You could go into woodcraft and do forestry work or do anything.

Mr Garrett came along on the first Monday with a lorry, shouted out names and said we all were going to Mr Eddy's farm. We all climbed in the lorry, dropping girls at different farms and then we were dropped at Mr Eddy's farm at St Erth. This was the first time we were introduced to a long-handled spade when we were sent on to plant cauliflower. They call them broccoli down here. We planted cabbages for three weeks. For the first few days everyone had blisters on their hands and heels. Everyone had plasters on due to the boots rubbing. We were a sorry lot.

I did some most peculiar jobs on some farms – rat catching, I dug drains and sewers all sorts of things, there was not a job I would not tackle, I really loved it.

One of the girls had an injury in her car. So he said to us, 'Would any of you like to drive?' and I said, "Oh yes, please."

– *Micky Bowman, Penzance*

Mary Quick writes:

After six weeks' training the girls had to go their separate ways. Betty was sent to Penzance, staying at Kenegie for about two weeks, then on to Treveglos farm at Zennor, where real farming was undertaken. Although wages were low considering the working hours, they were an improvement on previous years. In the 1930's it was £1.10s, rising to £2.8s in June 1940 and £4 in June 1946. Treveglos, or Churchtown Farm, as it was better known, was indeed within touching distance of the church from which it derived its name. Maintenance of the pedigree Guernsey dairy herd was its first consideration, although feed crops such as corn and hay as well as cabbages, mangolds and turnips (before they were blamed for tainting milk) were grown. The requirements of war also meant that as much spare acreage as possible had to be given over to the cultivation of potatoes, with quotas set by the Ministry of Food.

LAND GIRLS: Londoner Pat came to Cornwall and stayed

Sheep went all ways as we herded them

A new film called The Land Girls, which was filmed in the Westcountry, opens later this year. Since we previewed the movie, readers have been keen to tell us what it was really like in the Women's Land Army. **DAVID GREEN** talks to Pat Peters

PHIL MONCKTON

● MEMENTO: Pat Peters, with the breeches she wore as a Land Girl (right)

AS a 17-year-old, Pat Peters caught a train from London's Paddington station in 1943 and headed for the far South West to become a Land Girl.

Reaching the end of the line at Penzance, she and other would-be Land Girls were loaded into a cattle lorry to be taken to the hostel where they were all staying.

Like many of the other girls from London, Pat, whose home was in East Dulwich, married and settled down. She and her husband Gordon live in retirement at Ashton, near Helston. They have two sons, Gary and Ashley, a granddaughter and two great-grandchildren.

After a month at Penzance, she was one of 20 girls herded into another cattle truck and taken to Wadebridge. Her first task was to spend eight hours picking potatoes.

"Weeks were spent at remote windswept places, potato-picking, hedging and clearing stones from waste ground. Boredom set in so we constantly devised ways to dodge work.

"We would keep up a relay of twos slowly walking to the furthest hedge of the fields.

"At the first sign of mist over Brown Willy we'd pray for rain and then be sorry when we got wet through and our lorry was nowhere to be seen.

"A day spent in a winter corn field to be cleared of thistles found our glamour girl 'Bunny' crouching in the stalks plucking her eyebrows, another girl writing poetry and another darning her socks.

"Some of us rubbed lipstick on to our arms and said we were allergic to this

tles. No wonder our foreman called us a lot of 'towny hellers'."

She and a friend were chosen to herd 20 sheep from Camelford to Tintagel, which left a trail of havoc in their wake. More than one garden lost its flowers, and clothes from a washing line were trampled on. "At a crossroads the sheep went all ways when some US trucks approached. Sheep, soldiers and both Land Girls ended up in a coal yard."

After 10 months, Pat was moved to a farm at Nancegollan, near Helston, where she met a young farmer and married him.

"Many days were hard work and tears were shed, but it was so much fun," said Pat, who remains friends with Land Girl pals Pauline and Kay. "We visit each other regularly and reminisce on those

The Western Morning News, March 18, 1998

The Women's Timber Corps

At camp, we spent four weeks at training, learning to use axes, billhooks, bow and cross-cut saws, how to sharpen and take care of our tools and to distinguish one tree from another. At the end of our training we were sorted out into General Foresters and Measurers.

Timber was needed for pitprops, cut into lengths of 9 ft, 6-½ ft and 4-½ feet to be used in the mines that produced the coal for our munitions factories. It was also needed for aircraft frames (quite a lot of these were made from wood) and some of the timber was used in the gliders that went to Arnhem.

Timber Corps Measurers assessed the available timber and would then talk to the landowners and farmers to agree a price for felling and removal. We, the General Foresters, would then make a road up to the wood with the bar off-cuts from the local sawmill and cover those with tons of sawdust. We had to do this, because in the winter, when the conditions made the ground so soggy, the lorries would get bogged down. We often then worked up to our knees in mud.

The heaviest job was loading 9-ft. pitprops. The 6-½-ft. props could be swung between two girls onto the lorry and some of the stronger ones could manage them on their own. However, the 9-fts. were a different thing altogether. Even the men had to use a lifting system employing bolsters, iron hoops holding front and back 'gaggers' and poles to create the loads.

Other Timber Girls (or Lumber-Jills, as we were then called) worked in the sawmills, cutting timber into whatever was required.

– "Pat Parker's War"

Boconnoc 1943
Promotion from measurer to sub-firewoman meant a rise in pay of 5s a week but this was "lost" in price of the billet found for me. This was about 2 miles from Lostwithiel on the Liskeard Road and I was transported the five miles to work by one of the lorries bringing workers from Lostwithiel – so I was able to get to know them. But I soon found another billet within walking distance – dear old Mrs Dunster, at East Lodge Cottage, agreed to take me as a boarder and looked after me

well (she was 84!). The cottage had no electricity, and water was available from a pump outside. A wooden shed down at the sawmill seconded as an office, and most of my time was spent there, though I enjoyed some forays into the woods with my four WTC measurers to measure the fallen timber. There is a chapter about it in my "Timber Corps Diary," which is in the manuscript section of the British Library.
– Vera Lloyd, New Zealand

My work was in the Forestry section, as a Land Girl, and we had a nearby camp of land workers who worked with us. I was 17 when I started in 1940, and we used to cut down trees in a 90-acre wood, with cross-cut saws, before cutting them into different lengths for pit props.

– C J Barriball, Holsworthy, Devon

My Timber Corps training in May 1943 was at Wetherby, Yorkshire (not far from home), where we were introduced to all aspects of forestry. Some of it was extremely hard, some not so hard – but it was so very, very different from 'civvy street' that its interest was guaranteed. My first posting was in the village of Evershot, half-way between Dorchester and Yeovil in Dorset, but then early in 1944 we were moved on to a camp at Boyton, outside Launceston, in Cornwall. It felt strange to be in a camp again after eight months in private billets, just the two of us, but good to have more company at both work and play. Here in

Dutson Wood, near Launceston, 1944-45. On the left is Jeanne Mason.

Dutson Wood, 1944-45

Dutson Wood, our work was felling with axes and saws, trimming out and the inevitable bonfires, and then sawing the felled timber into the appropriate measurements either to be left as timber or for pitprops for the mines.

Crosscut and bushman saws were used in these operations, but sometimes the whole tree would be sawn on portable sawbenches with a team of five or six heaving it up and pushing it along. I always seemed to be on the thin end which took all the weight until the timber was halfway through the sawing!

It was hard work, but we were all in the same boat, and eventually, my friend Pat and I got over our aches and pains and got on with the job in hand. I can't remember too much detail about pay, but I do remember that we were on piecework, mainly, I think, to make sure we didn't shirk! Our 'felling rate' was 1/-d between two of us for soft woods and 2/-d for hard woods which included trimming off the branches and burning the 'tops.' We were not on the same job every day, so luckily at the end of the week our pay levelled out. Had we been felling every day I don't think I would have made it to the first weekend but, having said that, we were quite pleased with our early efforts when we felled 11 trees between us, and earned the princely sum of 11/-d!
– *Jeanne Mason, Leeds, Yorkshire*

After a month a man came from Truro, pointed at some of us and said we had to get into another cattle lorry up to Wadebridge. We were in for a shock then; we had to be at the church each morning to get in a lorry at 8, so had to be up at 7, and then into the fields at Tintagel and all up the north coast. Plenty of saints up there, picking up potatoes, potatoes, potatoes! It was all right in the sunshine – we had to pick up stones first as they could not plant potatoes in a stony field.

After 10 months we got really fed up with this, so we sat in a ring, put the stones in a heap and decided we were going to sign a petition to say we would go back to London, we had had enough. One of the reasons we were called the "towny hellers"! So the foreman said, "Dear, dear, dear, we can't do without you girls, we need the food, the potatoes, we need you." So he said he would see what he could do. We were all billeted to private farms and I went back to Nancegollan.
– *Pat Peters, Helston*

As a young girl, named Marjorie Spencer then, my mother was evacuated to Cornwall and stayed at Trewithen Terrace, Ashton, Helston. As school children they were allowed to work two days a week for local farmers helping to harvest their crops. Because they were so poor they often skived off to work in the fields to earn extra money, many times being caught and sent back to school. Though not a Land Girl, she knew well of their work.
– *Dennis Baylis*

Cornishman and Cornish Telegraph,
April 16th, 1941

Letter from S H Eva
of Roseworthy Barton, Camborne

"Women and the Land"

Sir – You all know me as an advocate of intensive farming to grow more food for the people; more pigs, corn, potatoes, broccoli and sugar beet… At present we all feel that we have already a larger programme than can be carried out to the best advantage with available labour. Has the possibility of employing women to supplement the work of our key-men had due consideration?

In July of 1916 I could not get labour to lift potatoes when the price was good. After the Land Army started I employed from 20 to 28 girls, and through 1917 and 1918 they helped to grow 40 acres of potatoes and 100 acres of broccoli each year. Many of the girls helped in the harvest, and some of them could build loads of corn like men.

Again we are at war, and every farmer is anxious to pull his weight to the uttermost. Last year not enough girls could be obtained for the Land Army. With the registration of women now about to take place there may be hundreds who will be glad to work on the land for the summer. It is essential that women should do everything on the land that it is possible for them to do, and so increase the total output of food produced by our key-men. For our farm we have already applied for 20 girls for sugar beet, potato and broccoli work. It is well to send in applications for girl labour at once in order to take advantage of the opportunity given by the coming registration. Write to Mrs Clifford Smith, 2 Farley-Terrace, Truro.

Enemy action:
One day we were out in the field cutting and stacking corn – we were lucky enough to be bought a big, red, brand-new Massey Ferguson tractor, not many people were so fortunate. Suddenly out of nowhere came a bomber.

It was German and was probably getting rid of leftover ammunition before going back home. Everyone dived into the uncut corn as quickly as possible and waited. When it had left, we all came out again. No-one was killed, but people in the houses nearby were injured. Penzance was bombed a few times, but apart from that it was very quiet down here. We never found much out about what was going on elsewhere.
– Ann Skewes, Coverack

I arrived at Truro in January '43 for a month's training on a smallholding at Carnon Downs, having been so keen to join. I kept telling myself I was enjoying it, but hoped the war would soon end. When I got to St Hilary Vicarage life certainly took a turn for the better. There were about 60 of us all packing our sandwiches, which my friend and I thought were salmon, though all the others had identified as sour pork. We had no ill effects. I learnt to milk the cows, drive an old Fordson tractor, and cut my fingers frequently lopping (cutting the leaves off) mangolds.
– Vera Searle, Rosudgeon

Cornishman, November 12th, 1941

Demonstration by
Cornish Girls

Girls of the Western section of the Cornwall Women's Land Army gave a demonstration of their efficiency in ploughing, hedging, hoeing, and planting at Polstrong Farm, Camborne, on Tuesday.

In the words of one prominent local farmer, the girls showed evidence of fast-approaching competence.

The winner of the cup for the most points was Miss F Bourne and the runners-up were the Misses D Bourne, M A Batten and A Bill.

The cup and prizes were distributed by Lt.-Col E H W Bolitho (Lord Lieut. Of Cornwall and chairman of the County Council) whose daughter Miss Ann Bolitho, one of the pioneers of the movement in Cornwall was among the prizewinners.

Where I lived at Oaken Lodge, Ashill, near Camborne, one field away there were decoy lights because Nancekuke Air base was near. One night a British plane landed in a field just opposite our bungalow with engine problems. Some Irish fusiliers came to guard it for about three weeks, and the officer asked my mother if she would warm their food and make tea for them. So each day and evening before bed time they would come in turn, two at a time, and have a cup of tea and a chat. One soldier's family is still our closest friends.

One night we heard a German plane and a British plane pass over, and there was a horrible noise when the British plane shot the other down over the North Cliffs. We were safe again. The Home Guard was always out in the evenings protecting Cornwall.

– Bessie Smith, Helston

I lived at the farm and the farmer and his wife treated me as a daughter. We milked the cows by hand starting 7 o'clock each morning. Then bottled milk as we took the milk to schools at Newquay. Then we washed all the bottles ready for the next day. After lunch it was cleaning out the cows and pigs houses. We grew cabbages and broccoli, carrots and potatoes. I remember many times packing them in crates when it was raining and very cold. I learnt to drive both the tractor and the

car. I also did a milk round: it was in 10-gallon churns and had to be measured. Then bottles came in, and made it a lot easier. Before I left to get married we had a milking machine installed. What a joy! No dirty tails in your face as you sat milking.

– Doreen Yelland, Truro

Before April 1944 I lived in London and was a shop assistant in Leicester Square. I had always loved the country and as I approached call-up age I decided to volunteer for the WLA, was accepted and first came to Praze, where a group of us were trained as rat catchers by Donald Bloomfield. On May 16 we went to Mullion with three others, a van and equipment, and proceeded to different farms trapping and poisoning rats. We enjoyed the countryside and life. I met a young man who worked for his uncle on a farm. The Land Girl there was leaving to get married and he offered me the job, which was to wash milk bottles, fill them after milking, cutting and weighing butters, marg, etc. rations and delivering to the homes. I also helped in the fields with potatoes and broccoli after the milk rounds finished. I should say that the young man and I got married 59 years ago and have lived in Mullion ever since.

– Elsie Hendy, Mullion

Edith Hocking at Portloe, near Veryan

Everywhere on this "cold comfort" Devon farm was slurry, inside and outside the cow and hen houses, and if one walked too fast it slopped up inside your wellies. Even the bucket of water for handwashing before and after milking (when there was one available) quickly became a deep greeny-yellow.

One of my first duties was to help in the (illegal) slaughtering of two pigs, manhandled out of their miserable lean-to of distintegrating galvanised iron sheeting and plastered with slurry and slime. I had to hold the wheelbarrow steady as one by one two men lifted and threw each pig into the barrow with its head over the end whilst a third man, after several attempts, slit their throats from ear to ear. That put an end to the poor creatures' heartrending screaming, but then the dreadful gurgling as the blood gushed out onto the stone yard of the dairy where the executions took place.

Moving on to my next farm – a lovely farm near St Merryn, Padstow, farmed by the Bennett family – on a temporary basis – was utter bliss.

– Polly Walker, Penzance

At Penzance Station I made a friend who has remained a friend to this day. We were based at Kenegie and then both assigned to a farmer near Tremethick Cross, at a farm which I believe is still going. Knowing that we were raw recruits, our first job was planting spuds. The horse and cart were made ready with a young farm hand holding the reins. We were helped up on either side and then he jerked the reins. The horse shot forward and we shot back onto the trays of spuds.

After a large group of Welshmen arrived, we were all moved on to different hostels. My friend and I went to Poltair and worked at nearby Trengwainton picking violets, then there was a farm at Trythall so here I used to ride my bicycle to and fro, did all sorts there, milked cows, haymaking, planting cabbage and also went to North Cornwall on a spud spring and then the winter stayed near Newquay.

– Dot Wylie, Penzance

THE LAND GIRL

WAR-TIME ADAPTABILITY

IT is perhaps fortunate that women have a greater gift for adapting themselves to circumstances than men, for it is on them, in war-time, that the heaviest burden of change falls. The man in the Forces? Yes. He has to adapt himself to complete change. But that is easier than coping with the continually differing aspects of the old life. Making-do with remnants of life as it was before the end of 1939 calls forth all the ingenuity and practicality of women.

It is everybody's first duty to save. For economy of clothing coupons I think that the best idea is to concentrate on preserving the clothes one already possesses, and buying the best one can afford when the necessity arises. The girl who wears a uniform should find this fairly easy. I have not bought a pair of stockings for over two years. I keep one very good pair for absolute best, otherwise I wear woollen stockings or ankle socks with costumes or slacks. Always slacks in the house, to save my better clothes, and nearly always slacks for wearing outside in summer. Cotton frocks on very hot days and bare legs. Uniform for going out in winter. All my old narrow-skirted frocks of a few years ago I have turned into working shirts and made knickers from the skirts. I have made a vest from the best parts of a blue silk shirt for wearing under thin blouses. Handkerchiefs can be made easily from parts of clothes cut up for other things. Mittens, fingerless gloves and short boot-socks from men's worn out socks and Land Army stockings. Dungarees patched at the knees with the cut-off bib, the waist put on to a band made of the straps. Converted pair of men's flannels for cooler summer days—pockets very useful. I have also discovered that an old evening frock will make a slip and knickers. Worn skirts can often be quite simply unpicked and "turned."

We have found several foods that are new to us. Among wild foods there are elderberries for pies and, dried, for currants, and lepiota and beef-steak—two types of fungus which we gather in season. The beef-steak grows on trees and looks like its name and the lepiota is a kind of mushroom of a creamy colour. We have tried dandelion coffee and herb tea—neither very exciting but nevertheless a change and a saving of rations. We eat horse meat—very tasty—especially steak and kidney pie. As for soya-bean flour—that is a definite discovery, for, with a little almond essence it makes a remarkable substitute for almond paste and can be used in very many other ways—sweet or savoury. We now cover the egg situation by keeping a few hens in our garden in a converted summer-house and put a considerable number in preserve for when they go off laying.

For soap, in the kitchen and bathroom, we have instituted soap dishes with holes and use the soapy water drained off to help in washing rough articles. When washing my hair I *always* use rain-water and keep each rinsing of water for washing clothes. I do all clothes washing in soft water as it saves the soap by half. (It also saves a lot of the tea ration if available for drinking.)

I have not used face-cream for well over a year now but have instead a little bottle of glycerine and rose-water which is lasting indefinitely, for a tiny touch of it spreads all over the face and holds powder marvellously. I only use powder on Saturdays and Sundays—if I go out. Lipstick I must have all the week. If one is used to lipstick one must always wear it for the sake of morale! It is still quite easy to obtain — of a sort and at a price!

Hair curling is a problem. I have made a few curlers with a piece of copper wire cut into short lengths to replace ones that have broken. I roll my hair upwards round a ribbon and if I help this to stay up with pins on damp days it goes two or three days without curling. I have two shorter, flat curls on the side of my head and these I keep so firmly, though invisibly, pinned down that even the rain cannot harm them. I keep an old Land Army hat for really wet days.

My hobbies and leisure times have not changed much. Before the war they were amateur dramatics, writing, music, reading and occasional pictures. Amateur dramatics have now changed to the activities of a local writer's circle. My occasional extravagances are books and magazines. While I was isolated in the country at one of my jobs, I bought a concertina to fill the place of the piano, which I missed. There is a piano where I am living now, but I am afraid it gets neglected a little these days, as I am concentrating on writing and reading, to the exclusion of most other activities. In

2   April, 1943

We lived in a requisitioned large house and went out to work in groups to whichever farmer needed us. Some farmers were great, some not so great. One in particular told us to carry the milk churns to the collecting point at the end of the lane before he would sign our time sheets. The full churns were very heavy but the farmer insisted that we carried two churns between three girls, so we picked up the churns and carried them to the end of the lane.

The time sheets were signed and the farmer said, "Well, girls, I knew you could do it."

"Yes," we replied, "but these are the empty churns, the full ones are back in the dairy."

– Hannah Pascoe, Helston

MINISTRY OF AGRICULTURE AND FISHERIES.

2—6——19 41.

AGRICULTURE ACT, 1937.

DEAR SIR (or MADAM),

It is proposed to carry out an inspection of ~~your~~ *Col. Paynter's* dairy herd on *Wednesday, June 4th* 19.4.1... at..... a.m. / p.m. Will you kindly arrange for your milking stock to be tied up or in stalls for this purpose.

Yours faithfully,

....
Veterinary Inspector.

N.B.—If the Veterinary Inspector has not called within one hour after the time stated it may be assumed that circumstances have prevented the inspection from being carried out.

M5851/2035 3/38 250,000 (15) 692 C.S.Ltd

Form No. B215/TA

My first assignment was at a dairy. We had to fill the milk bottles and churns to carry and you'd get the odd one which of course you couldn't do. Also the tops of the bottle, one was red and the other blue, and the customers would ask which was the evening milk, because the cream had settled, and which was the morning? I didn't tell them because I would have been in trouble. I stayed at the dairy for about 14 months. Then I was shifted to a farm, near Launceston, or Lanson, as the locals called it. The farmer met me at the station and we drove to Pipers Pool about 20 miles away. The farmer's wife was very good to me and I was very happy there. They had a daughter roughly the same age as me and we got on well. I had to get up at 6:30 a.m. and milk the cows, with the farmer and his daughter. We got the churns outside the gate for the milk lorry to pick up and then we went in to a hearty breakfast. After breakfast we had the dirty churns to do. Cleaning out the cowsheds, then out to spread dung on the fields. When harvest came around I had to stand the stooks up, and if it rained overnight we had to turn them round.

– Iris Woodcock, Kent

Betty Clark, Queensland, Australia, writes:

I was about four years in the Land Army, and did my training at Cullarian near St Erth. Mostly learnt to milk cows. I had two dairy instructresses, and some fieldwork. After training I was sent to a farm at Flushing. It was not too bad - just not enough to do. I then heard that a permanent land girl at Cullarian was getting married so I went back.

Main duties: milking and milk round and all morning driving around Canonstown and St Erth in a Commer van, tipping the milk out of the buckets into pint measures. Not like nowadays. In summer time it was double duties, working from five in the morning until ten o'clock at night, in the fields as well. About 30 cows in our herd. When we arrived back at lunchtime I washed out the van until other duties were assigned. I didn't really have a social life. I lived in a caravan in the yard while my friend, Suzanne, lived in a shed. My husband-to-be was a prisoner of war in Italy and Germany. When he came home, I gave a week's notice and got married. I would do it again. It was good — I had been used to the country but we did have some girls who came down, hairdressers and all sorts; it was strange for them to get used to it.

ACHIEVEMENT IN FEEDING BRITAIN

Dutson Wood, 1944-45

A long service, 1941-49:

General farm work: Farmyard work, cleaning cows' houses. Stables, pig styes, etc. Planting cabbage and broccoli, hoeing, weeding. Driving horses in harrows, roller chain harrows. Corn and hay harvest time, stacking sheaves till ready for the rick. Tractor driving. Drove calves to Penzance Market in horse and cart. Led a cow around the ring in Penzance Market, and sold her.

– *Carol Josling, Ludgvan*

From the farmer's perspective:

We had six Land Girls at our farm. They stayed for a month's training, then left to go to other farms. Some picked up the farming very well, but some were not so good. One put the milking machine on a heifer and was kicked into the ditch. They were taught to hand-milk and machine-milk. Milking was finished before 8 a.m. then they had breakfast. Inspectors came to the farm to check the Land Girls were being trained properly. They did all aspects of farming except working the fields with horses.

– *Dilly Gear, Coverack*

Learning…

One of the Land Girls didn't know anything about the facts of life; we didn't in those days. She said to me, "I have to go with the farmer now, we have to take the bull to the cow." So we went, and the farmer said, "You stay outside, you girls are not to watch this." So we found a little crack and had a look through and she said to me, "Hum, if that's what happens I am never going to get married." It was good fun.

– *Sheila Ellis, St Austell*

CORNWALL WOMEN'S LAND ARMY

Tel:Truro 2958   W.L.A.Office,
                      2,Farley Tce.,
                      TRURO.

Dear Miss Simpson,

     I have very much pleasure in sending you a half-diamond in recognition of your *second* half year of satisfactory service with the W.L.A.

     We in Cornwall should very much prefer to present these "Good Service" stripes on some special occasion when we could be gathered together, but since the difficulty of transport and similar considerations prevent this, I am sending you now the congratulations of my Chairman, my Committee and myself, and our thanks for the good work you are doing.

     Yours sincerely,

     W.J. Clifford Smith

     (Mrs.Clifford Smith)
     Organising Secretary.

am also enclosing first ½ diamond which I understand you did not receive

My home was Cornwall, and my family were small farmers. I wanted to work on the land, and joined up at 17. I loved the cows. And I liked to drive the tractor, do the hay and chain harrowing with horses, even though the farmer said I was not going very straight. I grew potatoes, mangolds, broccoli and it used to be very wet sometimes. Then we would go into St Austell with them all crated up to send up to the London markets. Once, quite late at night, the moon was shining and I was out in a field hoeing. I looked up and it was so beautiful, I knew I loved it. I also went out at night to see to the lambs.

And the cows, I knew every one by name, but we did have foot-and-mouth disease and that really, really upset me. They had to destroy all them. It was six months before we could start to build up again. When the Land Army finished, I joined the Emergency Milking Unit and went all over the country, then ended up at an estate in Northampton as head herdswoman. I was 37 before I married.

– *Edith Hocking, St Austell*

A husband's pride in his wife's work . . .
I am writing on behalf of my wife, I shall attempt to give you as much information as possible regarding her WLA service. She joined early in the year of 1943 and remained until after our marriage in 1946. Her initial training was on a dairy farm in Hayle; one can imagine her first morning being introduced to a shed full of cows requiring to be milked, having never been near to a cow, then seeing them in a field out of a train window. A frightening experience for any young woman, I personally take my hat off to all the young girls who took part in what could be termed as an adventure in their young lives. Farm work was no picnic in those days, nowhere near the mechanics of today. She was directed to my place of employment, this being Tempellow Farm, St Keyne, near Liskeard. She had many duties there, for it was a stock-rearing farm. The cows were milked – and the milk separated to feed the young calves. There were many menial jobs, such as dung spreading. She and I spent hours out in the fields staking out by hand the heaps of dung that had been previously

put out in heaps by horse and cart. She was billeted in a private house some half-mile from the farm. Not all the Land Girls were privately housed.
– *Phyllis Perkins, St Austell*

Through the eyes of a youngster . . .
I was a young boy working on Trenoweth Farm on the Lizard. After the war I remember about a hundred girls coming to Dry Tree Camp near where Goonhilly Satellite Earth Station is now. The Land Girls stepped in until everyone had sorted themselves out after the war. They took over the army camps that the men had used during the war. So many men weren't fit to do any work when they came home.

The locals were very pleased to see the girls who never complained. There was a girl called Rose who would tackle anything. I remember June Halford, she came from London, we worked alongside each other all the time. She married a boy from Helston. I wonder what became of her.

– *George Watters, Coverack*

Photo from article about Land Girls in
The Daily Telegraph, March 12, 1994

WTC "lasses" from Boyton Camp,
Dutson Wood, 1944-45

In 1947 I was transferred to Lord St Levan's Home Farm in Marazion as dairy maid making butter, cream and cheese for the Mount. This was where I met my husband just released from the Army.
We were married for 50 years.
– *Violet Stevens, Marazion*

Based at Gunnislake, Seaton, Penzance, Isles of Scilly (Tresco). Learned all aspects of farming, milking, weaning calves, sending them to be slaughtered for veal, which I have never eaten from that day to this. Hoeing crops, cabbage, etc. I realized dairy farming was not for my friend Beattie and me. We decided that market gardening would be our future. At least we would have some Sundays away from work and not breaking our hearts over the animals we grew to love.
– *Ellen Knight, Birkenhead*

Ooooooooh, the rat catchers . . .
We had a Hillman van with a canvas roof and we had arsenic and strychnine, goodness knows what else in loose tins with lids in the back of the van – it could have killed half the population. People didn't touch things that didn't belong to them in those days. We had a long-handled spoon for pushing down rat

holes. Given names of farms had to visit, a man came with me who said, "You can drive." I was not familiar with lots of places, he gave me directions and we went to farms, put poison down and made sure no other animals would get at it. Got chased by cockerels and dogs and bulls and goodness knows what else. Two days later went back to pick up the evidence and then had to dispose of them all.
– *Mary Mitchell, Hayle*

I joined the Women's Land Army Rat Catchers on my 17th birthday (19 March 1942).
I spent three years rat catching around Cornwall working on farms, army barracks, American barracks. Unfortunately, once on a farm all the lovely white chickens, about 50, died eating the poison put down for rats. The farmer went quite mad.
The scariest time was when another Land Girl and myself were in a large field with armfuls of rat traps and a German plane went overhead throwing silver strips over us. We were miles from anywhere and expecting to be machine-gunned at any time.
It was fun when we worked in the American barracks. They complained of rats in the kitchen. Whilst we were putting the poison down they made us huge steak sandwiches.
Whilst working on the cliffs "gassing out" foxes/badgers I nearly gassed myself as I had to go down the very large hole.
– *Doreen Nile, Grampound*

We trained Italian prisoners to help out in the fields. After I married a farmer we had German prisoners working for us. One early morning a plane crashed just out of St Mawgan and the airmen bailed out in our fields. We looked after them until help arrived.

– Irene Karkeek, Newquay

There were also two German prisoners on the farm. They lived in one of the large sheds out in the yard. One of them left quite soon, but the older one, Hans, stayed on. He was a lovely fellow, about the same age as my own father.

We had a very large bull we had to feed, and Sedge (another Land Girl) and I used to feed the bull before we went in for our tea. One particular day, Hans said he would feed him for us, so off we went for tea when we heard screams and the bull going mad. We just looked at each other and then ran like mad to the bull's shed. Poor Hans was already on the floor and the bull was revving up for another charge. There was no time to stop to think, we just rushed in, grabbed poor Hans, and dragged him out, slammed the barn doors and collapsed on the ground.

We were lucky, the bull hadn't touched us, but poor Hans was rushed to hospital and was there for some time. Sedge and myself were very honoured. We each were presented with a large certificate in a lovely frame in "Recognition of Heroic Endeavour to Save Human Life – 2nd September 1946."

– Mary Pightling, Helston

Mary Keverne, Hannah Pascoe and Iris Ruberry, in Helston, 1945

CHAPTER 5

The Social Slice of Life

Though time for socialising was short for everyone, often amounting to a meagre half day a week off work, and sometimes none at all, especially at harvest time, opportunities were never wasted. Most of the girls had some leave during the year to go home and visit their families. Dances were arranged, and social occasions designed especially for the Land Girls were organised by the county committee. Competitions and demonstrations also gave rise to entertainment and relaxation. The newspapers were quick to report on happy occasions in the spirit of "positive thinking." Morale was high amongst the Land Girls.

Cornishman, October 15th, 1941
WOMEN'S LAND ARMY
Club at Penzance

A meeting of members of the Women's Land Army was held at Penzance, in a room kindly loaned by the WVS on Saturday.

The matter under discussion was the forming of a club for the girls in the West Penwith district, of whom there are between 40 and 50.

At the inaugural meeting it was decided to open the club from 2 pm to 4 pm on Saturdays, and each alternate Saturday from 2 pm to 5 pm. The aim of the club was that the girls could meet and discuss matters together.

Mrs Charles Williams addressed the meeting. She was supported by Mrs Clifford Smith, Truro (organising secretary for the county), Mrs E H W Bolitho (committee member for the area), Mrs Littler, Mrs Hall and Mrs John Bolitho (area representatives).

Photo: Joan Guntrip and Frances Cross,
Lower Sticker Farm, St Austell, 1949-50

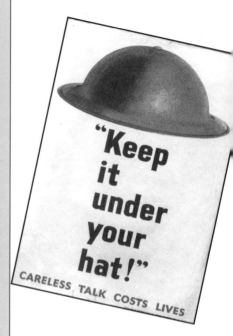

"Keep it under your hat!"

CARELESS TALK COSTS LIVES

Cornishman, February 4th, 1942

WEST CORNWALL NEWS
Canonstown

On Thursday a large audience were entertained by members of the Women's Land Army from the local (Colurrian) training center, who gave a programme of vocal items, including many favourites with choruses in which the audience joined lustily, and an amusing item specially adapted by the Land Army and depicting in song and action scenes during training. They were supported by Miss Nicholls and Mr W B O Tregarthen, the lady County Council Instructor and the owner of the training centre, the last named acting as chairman and compere. The concert party introduced by Mr F Kent was given an enthusiastic welcome. Their pianist was Miss Mary Carne, who was responsible for the concert arrangements. Solos were given by Miss Farrow, Miss Nicholls and Derrent, and Miss Farrow and Mrs Palmer. A trio was given by Mrs Williams and Misses Williams and Cocking. Others taking part in choruses were Miss J Nicholls, M Tapsell, P Keen and B Davy. Miss Betty Lane rendered unaccompanied items. The collection in aid of Mrs Churchill's Aid for Russia Fund realized £2 10s, was taken up by the Misses Joan Crawford and P Tamlin, members of the Land Army. The thanks of the meeting were accorded to the party, after which they were entertained to supper.

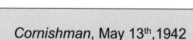

Keep mum she's not so dumb!

CARELESS TALK COSTS LIVES

Cornishman, May 13th, 1942

THE ROYAL VISIT AT LAND GIRLS' HOSTEL

An attractive scene

A sudden excitement among the sightseers on either side of the road, and the cry goes up, passed from mouth to mouth, that their Majesties are approaching the Women Land Army hostel at Ponsandane, which they are to visit and see the girls there. Cheering in the distance, getting nearer and nearer, and the Royal car, with roof drawn back, comes to a stand outside this recently-erected building.

At this hostel, set in green, shady surroundings, with a trout stream nearby that tinkles its Spring song down to the sea, their Majesties were presented to Mrs Charles Williams, chairman of the Land Army in Cornwall and Mrs Edward Bolitho, head of the committee. Here, assembled row on row were about 130 girls many of whom for years had been long in cities, but who were now helping to make Cornwall a greener land and a corner of the country that is providing much towards the nation's well being. To most of the girls work on farms was strange to them until they joined this service and a large contingent of them came from Lancashire with a sprinkling of Yorkshire, while one of them, Marjorie Martin, had been for a number of years in George Black's London revues and another who trod the stage before hostilities was Anne Cotton.

With cheeks aglow and bronzed by their war sojourn in the country, they presented an attractive sight, these Land Girls, to the King and Queen, who moved down every rank, stopping every few yards to ask questions and converse with this lass or that. All with whom they spoke declared themselves at home among the ploughing and sowing and reaping and mowing. Among the first to whom they spoke were Miss Anne Bolitho, daughter of the Lord-Lieutenant, and Miss Garland, daughter of a well-known Hayle farmer who, with Miss Blackwall and others, are Land Army veterans, having done two years' service. Present too was Mrs Clifford Smith, secretary of the Land Army in Cornwall.

Among the Land Girls present was Miss Phaby, who had won the Cornwall and Army Cup for her work, while among the many who were spoken to by the King and Queen were Elizabeth McKenna, petite brunette from Halifax, with lots of fuzzy hair; Joan Harrison who told the Queen, "I like the work, fine"; Frances Windell of Liverpool; Joan Battersby; Mary Lord, of Waterfoot in Lancashire; Sarah Baggs, of Liverpool, to whom the King said: "This is a big change after a big town"; Norah Long, of Halifax;

Peggy Blomley and Connie Wright of London.

The King and Queen also engaged in conversation with Carol Rona Morkan of Penzance who is a Land Girl, employed at Boswednan, Tremethick Cross. The Queen asked her if she liked her uniform and if she were happy there. The King asked her if she wore her heavy shoes always and she replied that she wore rubber boots as well. The Queen said she was pleased that they were so happy and the King said that they were a smart uniformed lot.

I have been present at several functions attended by Royalty, but never before have I seen any member of the Royal Family pay so much attention and take so great an interest in this as their Majesties did while talking to and being told about these girls…Accompanying the King and Queen were Sir Hugh Elles and Lady Elles, Sir Alan Lascelles, Commander Harold Campbell, and Countess Spencer, who was Lady-in-Waiting to the Queen, and is chairman of the Women's Land Army in Northamptonshire…

It was a great honour in May 1942 when the King and Queen came – they were down here on other business and came in the morning and inspected all the local Land Girls at Ponsandane, and spoke to some of us.
– *Lady Bolitho, Penzance*

The King and Queen visited Ponsandane Land Army Hotel. My friend and I were invited to stand in line with resident Land Girls where we were inspected. Stopping in front of me, King George asked me a couple of questions about uniform and such.
Carol Josling, Ludgvan

In the evenings we were all fed very well. We read, did knitting, and sang. Really it was a fun thing. Later on in the lorry they sang, and one or two girls had truly lovely voices. I never met a Land Army girl, certainly not in my neck of the wood, who was not happy and really loving it.

– *Mickey Bowman, Penzance*

Everyone carried on going to the cinema for entertainment, but if the siren went everyone would have to run out and down the street to the nearest shelter. When I was in the Land Army in Cornwall we would cycle into Penzance for the cinema, or get a bus in winter. Because we didn't have televisions then, we didn't really know what was going on away from our areas. No-one talked about it either. The posters everywhere warned us:
"Careless talk costs lives."
– *Ann Skewes, Coverack*

Joan Guntrip and Frances Cross, Lower Sticker Farm

There was a Forces canteen in Market Jew Street that would allow Land Girls to have a cup of tea. Not so in NAAFI. I remember the Motor Torpedo Boat (MT boats) especially because the sailors would dance with us. They treated us with appreciation for the work we did. They knew what it was like to be away from home and creature comforts.
– *Ellen Knight, Birkenhead*

I had always walked in my sister's shadow because she was absolutely stunning looking and I suddenly found that people wanted me. Of course, I had the great advantage of playing the piano. We didn't have records then and if they wanted to dance they had to come to me. Two of us played but the other was a classical pianist, whereas I would play jazz. Everyone in the NAAFI and YMCA knew me. I was in great demand for the first time in my life. So it was not only the farm work that mattered. It was also the social life and we lived as Gulval residents. If someone died we followed the funeral. If someone got married I played the piano for the dancing. So I feel we had a slightly different Land Army life. We were invited out to tea by the villagers every weekend.

And, I met the King and Queen. Someone said, "George and Liz are coming." The next day we all lined up, Land Girls came from all over Cornwall. Three of us were without our uniforms, and so they put us right at the back. The King and Queen came in and spotted us immediately and came to us. The King said, "Where is your uniform?" I said, "It hasn't come through yet." And the Queen asked, "Will you wear it when it does?" That evening it was on the door step and it was a superior uniform.

And I also met Lady Denman, the head one – the WLA was her idea, and she was head of the WI as well. I spent the day with her.
– *Rita Smith, Falmouth*

Lower Sticker Farm, St Austell

Although I was not old enough to be a wartime Land Girl, I did service from April 1949 until the Land Army disbanded in 1950 and would have stayed on in Cornwall but for a knee injury that put me out of action. My friend, Frances Cross and I made the most of our "sit up and beg" bikes and headed for the beach after work during the summer. The Saturday night dances, with live music, were quite something and if we missed the last bus back, it meant hitchhiking back to Sticker.
– *Joan Brown*

Had a Young Farmers' do down there and all these young farmers came to plough and do different things. That is where I met my husband in a cowshed. The cows had been milked and the other Land Girl had to clean it out. And these chaps were saying we will help you. We said, "Clear off," and in the end it got to be a throwing match of water. That evening we went to a dance, and here we are!
– *Pat Peters, Helston*

We had an army camp in the village (in Essex), and had dances. There were enormous American air bases and the American lorries used to come into the village and load us all into the back of the lorries with, I have to say, very fierce chaperones. We were taken to air bases for dances. Then the chaperones would count us all back at 11 o'clock.

– *Ann Foreman, Hayle*

It was great, wonderful comrades and it was just a good life. Of course, it was not so good in the winter when ice was on the broccoli. But, we didn't get up too early and worked in the evening only when we wanted to. We had a good social life and had a dance hall in Helston where we all went. We had a NAAFI and were always welcome there. If there were any bad times we forgot them. We only remember the good times. There is still a group around Helston that meets regularly. With one of them I have been friends for over 60 years. We are still firm friends and meet up every week without fail.

– *Hannah Pascoe, Helston*

When we had time off, we would cycle into Penzance (from Sennen) and perhaps go to the cinema. There were troops stationed all around us and they would invite us to dances, which we loved, and we would go often for lovely evenings dancing to Glenn Miller records. Some of the local girls were a little jealous of us because we might have taken their boyfriends.

There were lots of troops and lots of dances, because the RAF and Army boys never knew when they were coming back. Their philosophy was to live for today as tomorrow might never come. People were generally good-natured and everyone helped each other. There was a good sense of comradeship and sharing, and many life-long friendships were formed, not to mention romances!

The best part of my time at Sennen was meeting my to-be husband, Stanley. When we met I was working with ponies and a horseshoe came off one. I kept the horseshoe, and later, Stanley, who owned a haulage company, put the horseshoe on the front of his lorry. It is still a cherished possession.

– *Ellen Prowse, Sennen*

I loved my time in the Land Army – I loved it, and all the Land Girls were lovely and it was a different life than it is now. Nobody got pregnant. I mean, I was four years in the Land Army and nobody got pregnant. Nobody was promiscuous. We weren't that type of people. We didn't know about things. We were still girls when we joined up.

– *Mary Keverne, Helston*

Menu 3 Braised Meat
[Cooking time, 2 hrs.]
Potatoes, Mixed Root vegetables, Watercress

Steamed Ginger Pudding

Utensils required:
Large saucepan and steamer; basin for pudding.

Recipes:

BRAISED MEAT

1 oz. fat, stewing beef (approx. 2 lb.), seasoning, 1½ lb. mixed root vegetables, 1 pint liquid: stock or water.

Roll meat or trim into neat pieces. Heat fat, brown meat on both sides. Remove meat from pan. Add vegetables, and mix with the fat. Add the liquid, then place meat on top of vegetables. Season well. Boil gently for 2 hours.

STEAMED GINGER PUDDING

8 oz. flour, 2 oz. fat, 1 level teaspoon bicarbonate of soda, 1 teaspoon ginger, 1 tablespoon treacle, milk to mix. Rub fat into flour, add bicarbonate, treacle, ginger and enough milk to mix to a dropping consistency. Put into a greased basin and steam for 1½ hours.

Note.—The remains of the meat may be eaten cold with salad or made into savoury dishes.

Method to have dinner ready by 1.p.m.

11 a.m.   Heat fat in large saucepan, brown meat on both sides: remove meat, add vegetables and stock, and place meat on top.

11.15 a.m.   Make ginger pudding. Put pudding on to steam in the steamer over the meat.

12.30 p.m.   Put 1½ lb. potatoes on to steam above or round the meat. and other vegetables.

1 p.m.   Dish up—sprinkle root vegetables with well-divided watercress.

Menu 4 Vegetable Stew with Sausage Meat Dumplings
[Cooking time, 35 minutes.]
Coffee Custard

Utensils required:
1 Saucepan.

Recipes:

VEGETABLE STEW WITH SAUSAGE MEAT DUMPLINGS

Stew: 1 or 2 sliced onions, 1 or 2 quartered tomatoes, 1 cup chopped celery, 1 cup diced carrots, 1 small diced turnip, 1 cup diced potatoes, 1 teaspoon salt, hot water to cover.
Dumplings: 4 oz. flour, ½ teaspoon salt, ¼ teaspoon baking-powder, 1½ oz. chopped suet, 1 dessertspoonful chopped parsley, ½ lb. sausage or sausage meat.

Boil water and add vegetables. Cover and cook for 15 minutes. Then add the potatoes, salt and pepper, bring to boil. Make the dumplings—mix together the flour, salt and baking-powder. Mix in the suet, add the parsley, and sausage, form into dumplings, and put into the stew. Cover and cook for 10–15 minutes.

COFFEE CUSTARD

3 dried eggs, dry; 1½ oz. sugar, 1½ pints milk, 3 level tablespoons flour, 2 dessertspoonsful coffee essence. Add sufficient milk
Mix together egg, flour, sugar and coffee essence. Add sufficient milk to make into smooth cream. Boil remaining milk—pour on to cream stirring well. Return all to pan—boil 3 minutes. Serve cold.

Method to have dinner ready by 1.p.m.

Preparation: Wash, peel and prepare the vegetables. Make the dumplings.

12.25 p.m.   Make coffee custard and put aside to cool.
12.30 p.m.   Make vegetable stew.
12.45 p.m.   Add dumplings.
1 p.m.   Dish up.

In my free time I painted – a young German spotted me and we became friends. Fred was 24 and was on holiday. He was a German Jew from Leipzig and had escaped with his three sisters to England a month before war was declared. His parents couldn't get away and were destined for the gas chambers. It was a terrible time for them. Herta, his eldest sister, settled in London and taught history at a university while the others finished school. They all did so well and I still hear from Fred – we have kept in contact all these years! He must be 85 – three of the family went to Canada. They were a charming family, hard working and intelligent. Forty years later we met in New York – it was quite romantic.

Then the Yanks came to train in Cornwall – they marched through the villages handing out chocolate and gum, which our little bombed-out baby gratefully received, being nearly 4 years old by then, and she patiently waited for them to pass by – sitting on a wall. "Hiya, Red" they'd call to her and load her up with sweets (she was a lovely redhead). Every Saturday there was a village "hop." Dancing to an accordion in the village hall – everybody came and it was great fun. One night some black soldiers came and they were so well mannered and charming to everyone.

The doctor's wife in the village organised a dance party once a month in a barn in the village with a lovely wooden floor. A dozen men, American, English, Canadian from different regiments and messes, were invited to come and the Land Girls brought food and the men brought wine. The Yanks taught us how to jive and jitterbug to all the latest Glenn Miller records and everyone had a wonderful time. There was no misbehaviour or drunkenness at all – just good fun. I met a charming staff sergeant called Bill, and I painted his portrait, then suddenly they all vanished – for the invasion had started. The Americans had a tough time and few got through, but Bill survived – but I got an airmail from him to say that he felt a complete heel, and hadn't had the guts to tell me he was married (my mother sighed with relief – but I was brokenhearted!) – so I sent off his portrait and that was that.

The fields around Perranuthnoe have so many lovely memories for me as a Land Girl – I returned four years ago – after an absence of 57 years (!) to find it just the same. The National Trust has taken over the coastline there and I was thrilled – it was like stepping into a dream.

– Joy Micallef, Germany

Though they ration petrol, tea or meat
I swear by Heaven above,

They never will or can control
That sloppy thing called 'Love'!

In my WLA days the birth of little calves or lambs even to a little chick pecking at its shell were most fantastic sights to see. Knowing when to teal the crops at different times of year is miraculous and the harvesting a wonder. The most awful experience I had was when a farmhand and I were shucking corn and we heard an aeroplane nearby. As we watched it was coming over the next field, then we heard gunfire. The farmhand had disappeared while I was still watching. I saw the pilot very clearly. The next noise was more gunfire across the valley in the farmyard, and then a volley of gunfire at Lostwithiel clockface.

Hence no mishaps.
– *Rita Pinhammer, St Austell*

Mary Quick writes:

During this time, Zennor was more isolated than usual; with petrol severely rationed, and outside interests could not be pursued as readily as before. The blackout alone restricted any great attempt at socialising. However, there was always the faithful bicycle, although much care needed to be taken with a very dimmed headlight, especially in dark country lanes, where it was prudent to ride in tandem.

Sometimes the chance came to be driven in a party to dance in St Ives, but in 1944 male partners were in short supply. U.S. troops who captivated local girls with their generosity and "jazz" sessions were already dying in France side by side with British servicemen. On some farms, prisoner-of-war Germans and Italians had been arriving steadily as the Allies progressed to victory, but they were not supposed to fraternise. In any case, it would have been difficult, seeing that they were housed in camps and driven to various farms during the day. Some of these young men were from farming families themselves, and were found to be of great assistance, especially the Italians, who were happy to have left the war behind. On clear evenings they were often to be heard singing their native songs across the valleys. Others, including hard-line Fascists, were not so accommodating and arguments could easily break out.

Young Farmers' clubs, though, were still a means of social communication, enabling Land Girls around the area to meet local youngsters. The eldest son of a farmer was exempt from call-up, so there was at least a small number who had left their teenage years behind, and many of them, most sensibly, eventually married Land Girls.

I recently saw a film called *The Land Girls* (1998), which people had told me was very good and that I would enjoy it being ex-WLA myself. Well! I watched it, and I must say, it was quite an enjoyable piece of entertainment, but Land Girls they certainly were not. We worked far too hard and too long for steamy romances with farmers' sons – even if there had been any. Most of them had been called up. If there had been one around we'd have been far too sleepy to bother.

Bed to us meant SLEEP.

– Sheila Ellis, St Austell

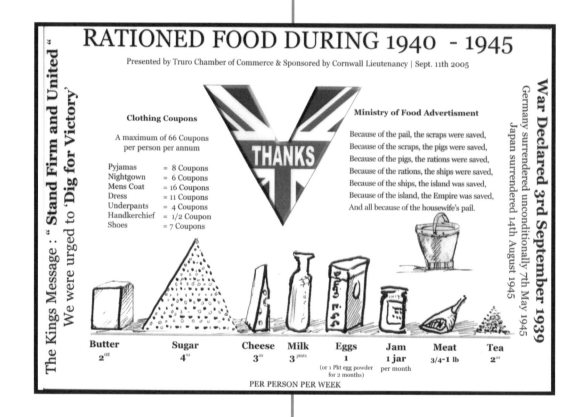

RATIONED FOOD DURING 1940 - 1945

Presented by Truro Chamber of Commerce & Sponsored by Cornwall Lieutenancy | Sept. 11th 2005

The Kings Message : " Stand Firm and United "
We were urged to 'Dig for Victory'

Clothing Coupons

A maximum of 66 Coupons
per person per annum

Pyjamas	= 8 Coupons
Nightgown	= 6 Coupons
Mens Coat	= 16 Coupons
Dress	= 11 Coupons
Underpants	= 4 Coupons
Handkerchief	= 1/2 Coupon
Shoes	= 7 Coupons

THANKS

Ministry of Food Advertisment

Because of the pail, the scraps were saved,
Because of the scraps, the pigs were saved,
Because of the pigs, the rations were saved,
Because of the rations, the ships were saved,
Because of the ships, the island was saved,
Because of the island, the Empire was saved,
And all because of the housewife's pail.

War Declared 3rd September 1939
Germany surrendered unconditionally 7th May 1945
Japan surrendered 14th August 1945

Butter	**Sugar**	**Cheese**	**Milk**	**Eggs**	**Jam**	**Meat**	**Tea**
2^{oz}	4^{oz}	3^{oz}	3^{pints}	1 (or 1 Pkt egg powder for 2 months)	1 jar per month	3/4-1 lb	2^{oz}

PER PERSON PER WEEK

CHAPTER 6

Victory! Back to Civvy Street

*Eventually I married one of the brothers; the
other was already married. So coming from
London and knowing nothing about farming,
it was a wonderful experience.*
– Fay Beckerleg, St Ives

The Land Army girls lived up to expectations, much to the amazement and growing admiration of the farmers for whom they worked. By marrying into Cornish families, as a large number did, they brought varied ideas and interests into the county. Some rural areas where in-breeding had become a matter of expedience benefited in particular from an influx of new blood. Because of family connections, links were also established in many other parts of Britain, so further assisting Cornwall's adjustment to changes brought about by the recent conflict.

In late spring of the final seven months of my work, I was busy down here because of the new idea "Lend a Hand on the Land." Anyone who had been demobbed from other forces or were working in offices were encouraged to spend their week's holiday giving help on the land. They were sent a voucher for their train fare and encouraged to work on the land. I was asked if I would like to work at one of these camps, and it was St Anthony in Roseland – Place House – like a small mansion, it was quite magnificent. Just two drivers, another and myself, we met every train coming in from Truro every Saturday.

Camping was very good. Farmers would phone up and say, can you send five workers or whatever, and I would do that. The workers used to ask to work with their friends. I would take them out to their work assignments, and then work on the last farm.

One girl said at the end of the day her foot was hurting and when she took off her boot she had been walking around all day with a mouse in her boot. Things were always happening like this, and we had such fun. It was like a holiday camp, and there was entertainment in the evening. Everyone wanted a photograph so we all collected outside the House for photos to be taken with the campers. Everyone signed them.

I was engaged at the end of the camp, so I gave in my notice. I had been in the WLA just over two years and here we are, still together 58 years later.

When I left the Land Army I had to send my uniform back and that was it.

– Micky Bowman, Penzance

WOMEN'S LAND ARMY (ENGLAND & WALES)
RELEASE CERTIFICATE

The Women's Land Army for England and Wales acknowledges with appreciation the services given by

MISS JOAN PAMELA GUNTRIP

who has been an enrolled member for the period from

22nd March 1949 to 1st July 1950

and has this day been granted a willing release.

Date 23rd June 1950

WOMEN'S LAND ARMY.

I married an Irishman from Kilkenny who had been evacuated with his family to Penzance. I met him on his leave from Burma. I made lots of friends during that time in the Land Army, and when I came out I worked for Samson Hosking, at Lamorna, on daffodils. We went to London and made a film about it with Richard Dimbleby. It was called *About Britain*, and it was a live show . . . a long time ago in Lime Grove.

I think Land Girls were brave and hard workers. We never had no recognition, but I have been recognised by my friends, and after all, that's the main thing.

– Florrie Coogan, Penzance

"I'm doing my bit – but I need your help"

Give 7 days in Summer to insure against want in Winter

WRITE FOR LEAFLET TO THE DEPARTMENT OF AGRICULTURE FOR SCOTLAND. 15 GROSVENOR ST. EDINBURGH

PRINTED FOR H.M. STATIONERY OFFICE BY GEO. STEWART & CO. LTD. EDINBURGH

We just left the Land Army, and didn't know we had been treated any different to other girls. I didn't realise they had gratuities and civvy clothes and lots of thank you's, and they were allowed to march to the Cenotaph. We didn't know that. Not for years. I didn't think anything more about it until I met up with some more Land Girls who were trying to get us recognised. We were able to march in 2000 and marched every year since.

Life as a Land Girl: I would not have missed it for the world; it was great. Nothing has been hard since. People say we have worked hard and I think, "Oh yes, we certainly did." When you have worked from 4 in the morning to 11 at night, you certainly know all about hard work, and the aching that goes with it.

– Sheila Ellis, St Austell

We got married from there, where my husband was farming. I met my husband, Charlie, when I first came to Penzance and we have been married for over 60 years. He worked on the farm where I was working at that time, and later when I was moved, he cycled 19 miles from Bodrifty to the Lizard for our dates. He was a horseman, and I could not understand what he said a lot of the time. We had a lovely time really. It was hard work at times but we all got on. It was lovely being with a lot of girls.

– Vera James, Penzance

Aside from hostels in Yorkshire and Lincolnshire, where I worked as a hostel forewoman and driver, I also worked from the Old Rectory, St Columb Major and Truro Vean, Truro.

Also two holiday camps, one in Truro and Place House, St Anthony, Cornwall. The holiday camps were especially enjoyable, meeting people from all walks of life, all in all a very happy experience.

– Kay Polmear, Truro

I met my husband on VJ day. We celebrated and next to the YMCA was the Prince of Wales Pub. I was there with five girls and he was there, a Cornishman from the Royal Navy, a commando. So I stayed in Cornwall. I have a son who is in Hamburg, Germany. I have friends, and I enjoyed myself.

On the trucks we used to sing Land Army songs.
"They sent us down to Cornwall,
They said it was very fine.
They said the sun was shining.
It was raining all the time!"
I finally left the Land Army when I was told I was being sent to Worcester to join the Land Girls there. My husband said, "If you go, I know you won't come back." So we got married.

– Eileen 'Taff' Williams, Penzance

Digging for Memories

I married a farmer's son. Mr Wilfred Badcock, the farmer where I worked and a very nice man, gave me away when I got married. I met Ronnie, my future husband, at a dance in Goldsithney and could not understand him as he spoke very quickly. He said, "Can I take you home?" I could not understand what he said. He was a lovely man, lovely boy, working as a farmer and in the Home Guard. In 1945 we went to live in a cottage, no water, no electricity, no nothing, but it was home. We moved into the farm later. I really enjoyed my time in the Land Army. One Land Girl married an American soldier and I stood for her.

– *Agnes Jilbert, St Hilary*

At age 16-1/2 years I was called up in South Wales for war work in a factory, working on a capstan lathe. After 18 months mainly working nights all I longed for was fresh air, so I joined the WLA (1944), and was sent to

Bridgend to a big camp with 200 Land Girls. I stayed there about one year then moved to Helston in Cornwall. From a camp of 200 to a house of about 20 was different. American servicemen had been in the house (Lesley House, Lady Street) before us and they left graffiti all over the walls. They were officers, and we were surprised! Later I moved to Goonhilly.

My only day of high emotion was D-Day. Having worked for some weeks with other girls and German POWs in South Wales, we got to know each other pretty well despite being told we were not to fraternise with the enemy. On D-Day, out in the field, we went wild on hearing the news, but an older POW whom we called "Pop" went on his knees in the earth and prayed. He was from Dresden and had not heard from his family for three years. We all cried and prayed with them. It was the saddest thing we would all remember.

On VJ-Day I was going home on leave during the evening and all through the night; it was dark by the time we got to Plymouth and all the ships had lights and fireworks. Every city we went through, Exeter, Taunton, Bridgwater, everywhere, all lit up and fireworks.

I left the Land Army when we got married in December 1947. My husband was a blacksmith locally from Helston so I never went back. It is a regret I have, in some ways. I never planned not to go back. My plan was to return to Wales and I had things in the pipe line.

– *Mary Keverne, Helston*

By this time the war was coming to a close so I left for a short time to decide what I would like to do in the future. Both my parents were dead, and the rest of the family, much older than me, were wonderful at offering to find me good (boring) jobs, but I found out in the second week of my holiday that the WLA was not disbanding at this time, so I applied again to join. Asked could I go to Cornwall to work with flowers, which was agreed, and I finished up at St Hilary's Vicarage, in Goldsithney, working for Tomlin's at their daffodil farm for quite a long, happy time.

– *Mary Maddern, Plymouth*

Betty Clark driving the tractor in Wings for Victory Parade through St Austell

Betty Clark again at the wheel, at the Wings for Victory Parade in Truro

I was in the Land Army for two years. I had to resign because I got engaged to a farmer's son. We met when I went thrashing at his farm and his father had managed to get a small-holding for us to get married. We lived on one farm for seven years and another one for 34 years. We ended up living in Cornwall and I just went back home for holidays. In the end my parents came to live down here and my sister did as well. We thoroughly enjoyed and loved every minute of it, but like other Land Girls have said, we were not recognized. We were not thanked and we did not want thanks, because we were doing it for our country. But all the other services were recognized. They were thanked and received a gratuity. They seemed to have this, that and the other, and we Land Girls got nothing.

– *Alice Talling, Llantegos by Fowey*

I often wonder about one of my Land Army pals, a Yorkshire lass named Joan, who married a G.I. She went off to America with him so full of romantic ideas to live in the Bronx. She was the girl I found crying inconsolably on our first week on joining the WLA. I asked her what was wrong and she told me between sobs that it wasn't as she expected. I asked her what she expected? It appeared that she was inspired with the adverts for recruiting Land Girls – a girl lying on a cart load of hay enjoying freedom and sunbathing.
"Silly girl," said I.
– *Irene Watson, St Ives*

I grew up in Newquay, and during the war the town was alive with troops from all over the world as well as the RAF and WAAF's at St Mawgan, which was bombed. I joined the Land Army aged 18 and was sent to a flower farm in St Martin's, on the Isles of Scilly, to relieve a farmer to go to the Army. To get there I took a train to Penzance and sailed on the Scillonian. It was just a small fishing boat – not the fancy yacht they have today! It was a rough trip to St Martin's. I picked daffodils, narcissus and onions, and packed the flowers in boxes to be sent to Covent Garden in London. When I was given leave I decided to fly back to Penzance to avoid the rough sea voyage. I had never flown before and was terrified, little knowing in the future that my 15-year working career was with the airlines.
– *Peggy Thomas, Newquay*

In a nutshell:

I enlisted in the WLA in 1941, at the tender age of 17-1/2, and after a medical examination, was soon leaving my native Derbyshire for the Training Centre in the wilds of Cornwall. What a shock! Here, in spartan conditions, I was introduced to farm life, via milking, dairy work and vegetable growing. After several weeks training, I qualified as a Dairy Maid, and went to work on the Williams farm at Lower Roskestal, some three miles from Land's End, where we milked 50 cows by hand, grew vegetables and daffodils. Since I had my own bedroom and the use of the bathroom with hot water, this was bliss compared with the Training Centre.

The work was hard and continued from dawn until dusk, with just one day off per week, but the local Scottish Regiment who were camped nearby and some American troops provided a little entertainment and relaxation. I stayed in Cornwall until 1944, when I was transferred to Derbyshire to be nearer to my home, and to work for a titled gentleman, who owned a mansion on a vast estate. Here, I was in charge of the dairy, calves and poultry. I left the Land Army in 1945, married my boyfriend, and shared his life as a chartered aeronautical engineer. In September 2006 we hope to celebrate our diamond wedding anniversary.

– *Elsie May Wright, Isle of Wight*

No. 6, Volume 7.   SEPTEMBER, 1946   Price 3d.

TIMBER !

ON August 31st the Women's Timber Corps came to an end. The last four hundred and fifty members who are engaged on the operations of the Home Timber Production Department, will remain members of the W.L.A. until these operations are finished, although no longer part of a separate Corps.

From the beginning of the War, there were members of the Land Army doing forestry work and in 1942 the Women's Timber Corps was established as a special section of the W.L.A. with its own badge and its enviable green beret. At its peak period there were over 6,000 members in England and Wales and in Scotland.

Of all the jobs which women on the land have undertaken, it is the work of the Timber Corps which would probably have startled our great grandmothers most. Land girls like Bo Peep and the Pretty Maid who was going a-milking and the Goose Girl have been friends for many generations; but there have been no nursery rhymes or fairy stories about maidens who hewed down forests nor cautionary tales about young ladies who cut off their fingers owing to carelessness with a circular saw.

During the War, members of the W.T.C. have tackled every sort of job connected with woods and trees. They have driven tractors and locomotives hauling loads of timber up and (still more dangerously) down impossible gradients, they have steered motor boats towing rafts of logs across distant lochs, they have measured trees and cut them down and sliced them up and sent them off to be used as telegraph poles and pit props and sleepers and packing cases and charcoal for munitions. During 1942 it was estimated that some members of the Timber Corps were saving fifty tons of shipping space per year *each*.

The Land Army will miss the Timber Corps at its Rallies and parties, for the green beret contingent was popular in any procession and welcome at any festivity. All members of the W.L.A. will wish their sisters of the Timber Corps the best of luck in the future and will salute them for the fine trail they have blazed in the world of women pioneers.

M.A.P.

The end of her Timber Corps days:
Once the sawmill was running smoothly I was transferred into the district office in Launceston. The District Officer was my old friend the district foreman of Jacobstowe days, and my time was divided between filling in endless forms alone in the office and riding round with the D.O. on visits to the slowly diminishing number of operations in the district, still keeping a motherly eye on the sawmill at Boyton.

The war was over and we had denuded the country of its timber; now came the task of tidying up and of reinstating the various woods we had despoiled. For the first time since 1941 I found myself unhappy in the work; I missed the companionship and ripe good humour of the various gangs I had worked with, and the monotonous routine of form-filling became unbearable without the familiar interruptions and the busy noise of the sawmill. So, in May 1946 I rejoined the ranks of civilians, the richer by over five years of happy comradeship with the people of the West Country.

– *Vera Lloyd, New Zealand*

Pat Parker's, and the nation's, Victory Parade, held in London:

When the WLA came along there was a whole contingent of them, and at the back, one row of Timber Corps girls in their green berets. The crowds around me were all saying to one another, "Land Army, Land Army." I couldn't let my girls go by without some recognition for them, so as loud as I could I yelled, "HURRAH FOR THE TIMBER CORPS!" The girls looked up, but I don't think that they saw me. When I got down from my perch, people saw my uniform and wanted to know what I had done during the war.

Then several years ago, I tried to gather the girls together for a reunion, and in one letter, the writer told me she had been one of the Victory Parade girls, and went on to write: "It lifted our hearts as we walked along to have someone shout to us TIMBER!!" That was me over 45 years ago, and I was and still am very proud of what we were and what we did. It saddens me to know that so few people have heard about us, the "Lost Army of the Woods."

– Pat Parker, London

"The gang" at Boconnoc, near Lostwithiel, 1944 (photo courtesy of Vera Lloyd)

*And marching in that same parade was
a representative from Cornwall:*
My proudest moment was being chosen to
represent Cornwall in the Victory Parade in
London. The Queen Mother gave us an extra
smile as we all marched by. Long live the
Women's Land Army!
– Rita Pinhammer, St Austell

Land Army days, would we do it again? I
think I would. We learnt some rather choice
languages from some of the men we worked
with. It was an eye-opener, and it was educational in its way. Yes, I think I would do it again.
It didn't do us any harm. We got down to doing
it, and although we grumbled, basically we enjoyed it. It was quite a different way of life.
– Kate Morris, Falmouth

WOMEN'S LAND ARMY

...Cornwall... County Office

Tel. Truro. 2292/3½

EDW/SN.

2, Farley Terrace,
Truro.
3rd Oct. 1945.

Miss Morgan,
Chiverton,
Perranuthnoe,
Marazion.

Dear Miss Morgan,

This is to inform you that you have
been released from membership of the
Women's Land Army as from 4th October,
1945.

I have informed the Ministry of
Labour of this and should be glad if you
would call at your local office as soon
as possible.

Will you please return your Land
Army badge and uniform to this office in
a clean condition within 14 days, with
the exception of one shirt and one pair
of shoes, putting your name and address
inside the parcel. When you return your
great coat we will then send you a dyed
one for your own use.

P.T.O.

WOMEN'S LAND ARMY

...Devon & Cornwall... County Office

Tel: Exeter 56214.

10, Alphington Road,
Exeter.

13th April, 1950.

Miss J.P. Guntripp,
13, Graham Avenue,
Poltaire, St. Austell.

Dear Miss Guntripp,

I have pleasure in
enclosing an armband representing your one
year's good service with the Land Army.

I do hope you will continue
in agriculture long after the Land Army comes
to an end.

Yours sincerely,

Miss E.M. Bastin.
County Secretary.

P.S. The 2 ½ diamonds should be sewn on to the
armband to form a whole diamond.

In the memorable words of Betty Nicholls:
Each year farming repeats itself. I saw the war
through to the end on this farm. To the people
with whom I lived, and those who surround-
ed my life at the time, I belonged.

Photo courtesy of Agnes Jilbert.

Sixty Years On

Presented by Truro Chamber of Commerce & Sponsored by Cornwall Lieutenancy

VE-VJ DAY 60th COMMEMORATIONS

"Thanks For Our Future"

THANKS

TEA PARTY

Garras Wharf, Truro
(Next to Tesco Carpark)
Sunday 11th September 05

4.00 - 7.00

Edith Hocking

Ann Foreman

Agnes Jilbert

Violet Stevens

Alice Talling

Hannah Pascoe

Peggy Godding

Mary Keverne

Mary Mitchell

Mary Pightling

Betty Clark

Vera James

Desiree, Lady Bolitho

Phyllis Perkins

Pat Peters

Terry Hockett

Rita Smith

Micky Bowman

Kathleen Morris

Joyce Morcomb

Jeanne Bardsley

Florrie Coogan

Claire Leith

Olive Benney

Joan Goodman

Joyce Tooth

Sheila Ellis

Jean Thomas

Of course, there were many more Land Girls whose pictures we would like to have included here but were unable to reach or photograph in time for publication . . . .

Former Land Girls meeting at Helston Library to record their stories.

Costumed Land Army dolls became favorite mascots for groups who met up to reminisce.

Land Army display for VE-VJ Day 60th anniversary commemorations in Penzance.

Honour Roll of Land Girls in Cornwall

Contributing to this Study of the Women's Land Army 2005:

Jeanne Bardsley *nee* Swindell

C. J. Barriball

Fay Beckerleg *nee* Tast

Olive Benney

Betty Berriman *nee* Williams

Desiree, Lady Bolitho

Mildred "Micky" Bowman *nee* Ward

Joan Brown *nee* Guntrip

Betty Clark *nee* Cawood

Florence Coogan *nee* Mitchell

Kathleen Crispin *nee* Chilwell
(WMN Report)

Eleanor "Lena" Doidge

Sheila Ellis *nee* Mott

Gwen Finnemore *nee* Holford

Ann Foreman *nee* Magnus

Hilda May "Dilly" Gear *nee* Collins

Peggy Godding *nee* Churchward

Joan Goodman *nee* Tolladay

Ivy Gordon *nee* Gant

Elsie Grose

Lily Harris *nee* Harris

Elsie Hendy *nee* Leigh

Edith Hocking *nee* Minear

Evelyn James

Vera James

Agnes Jilbert *nee* Taylor

Carol R. Josling *nee* Morkam

Irene Karkeek *nee* Hurrell

Mary Keverne *nee* Rogers

Ellen Knight *nee* Gopsill

Ann Law *nee* Estride

Claire Leith *nee* Oats

Vera Lloyd

Mary Maddern *nee* Smith

Ada Martin *nee* Beare

Jeanne Mason

Joy Micallef

Mary Mitchell *nee* Emmott

Joyce Morcomb *nee* Harris

Joy Morgan

Kate Morris *nee* Goodger

Joy Mundy *nee* French

Dora Nicholas

Elizabeth "Betty" Nicholls *nee* Lane

Doreen Nile *nee* Tibbett

Marjorie Overton-Larty *nee* Whitworth

Hannah Pascoe *nee* Moscrop

Phyllis Perkins *nee* Jefferiss

Pat Peters *nee* Davis

Mary Pightling *nee* Addison

Rita Pinhammer

Kay Polmear *nee* Richardson

Ellen Prowse *nee* Ash

Lois Pulford

Barbara Roberts *nee* Farmer

Iris Ruberry *nee* Rees

May Schlesinger

Vera Searle *nee* Ranner

Leonora Simpson

Ann Skewes *nee* Morgan

Bessie Smith *nee* Teague

Rita Smith *nee* Waller

Phyllis Stern *nee* Gould

Violet Stevens *nee* Tippett

Alice Talling *nee* Peet

Jean Thomas *nee* Thompson

Peggy Thomas *nee* Wade

Thelma Thomas

Joyce Tooth *nee* Perry

Jean Trevaskis *nee* Thomas

Nancy Trevennen *nee* Johnson

Polly Walker

Irene Watson *nee* Nicholson

Peggy White *nee* Eastall

Eileen Williams *nee* Cullen

Verona Williams *nee* Luke

Jill Wilson *nee* Boswarva

Iris Woodcock

Elsie May Wright *nee* Goodwin

Dorothy Edith Wylie

Doreen Yelland *nee* Catt

Anonymous: 2

. . . and many others who came forward after we went to print.

Land Army girls writing to us from further afield, who worked with the WLA in Cornwall and elsewhere in the U.K.:

Mary Harrison *nee* Hibberd,
Harrogate, North Yorkshire,
who worked at Lamorna Cove

Mabel Irene Ogilvie *nee* Thomas,
Swansea

Joan Hawksworth *nee* Grimshaw,
Merseyside

Bea Ottiwell, Lancashire,
who was at Ponsandane & Varfell
Farm from 1942

Doreen Howlings,
Leeds

Pat Parker *nee* Champion,
Norbury, London

Jean Jones,
WLA in Herefordshire

Joyce Spicer,
Hampshire

Doreen Molloy,
Birmingham

Other welcomed correspondents:

Dennis Baylis, about his mother, **Marjorie Spencer,** who worked on the farms around Helston as a schoolchild.

Letter from the daughter of **Ethel Bird,** known as "Mary," who worked with the WLA in Perranporth, and married Patrick Cain from Penzance. (She died in 1957, aged 29.)

Patricia "Tricia" Harris, who was too young but worked on farms and knew Land Girls.

Liz Jupe, about her godmother, the late **Dora Nicholas,** and her work as an instructor in Cornwall.

Sally Lawrence, about her grandmother, the late Ann Skewes, who as Ann Morgan left London in 1942 and worked at Henfor Farm, Long Rock.

Debra Neave, for her aunt, the late Betty Mulholland.

Evelyn Paine, though not in uniform, worked on the farms.

W E Perkins, for his wife, Phyllis Perkins, St Austell.

Mary Quick, about her friend the late Betty Williams Berriman.

Elizabeth Sparrow, about the former use of her home as a Land Army hostel.

George Watters, who as a young boy worked on Trenoweth Farm on the Lizard and remembers the Land Girls stepping in after the war and staying until everyone sorted themselves out.

Peter Wood, remembering his youthful destruction of a Land Girl's cigarettes (he had never seen any before!).

Note to readers:
If there is anyone on this list whom you may wish to contact, please write to the Hypatia Trust, Trevelyan House, 16 Chapel Street, Penzance, Cornwall TR18 4AW, enclosing your communication. We will be happy to forward it to the person named, with their express permission. No addresses will be released to enquirers, as the Hypatia Trust adheres to a strict Data Protection policy.

We strove to accurately identify the many photos in this book, some of which we received third-hand. We apologize for any errors or omissions in identification. In addition, place names and spellings not only varied with different accounts, but, as is often the case in Cornwall, a place name may have three or four different spellings. Any confusion would be entirely understandable.

Bibliography

Acton, Viv and Derek Carter. *Operation Cornwall 1940-1944: The Fal, the Helford and D-Day.* Truro: Landfall Publications, 1994.

Acton, Viv and Derek Carter. *Cornish War & Peace: The Road to Victory – and Beyond.* Truro: Landfall Publications, 1995.

Age Exchange Theatre Trust. "What did you do in the War, Mum? Women recall their wartime work London." Third edition, 2000.

Clark, Betty. *Dragonfly On Tractor: My Years in the Women's Land Army.* Printed for private circulation in Queensland, Australia, 2002. This little book is about Betty Clark's life in Cornwall, primarily working at Cullarian, St Erth.

Johnstone, June. "Cornish Recipes We Ate Before, During, & After the Last War." June of Troon, 2004-05.

Lawrence, Sally. "World War II: An interview undertaken by the author with her grandmother, the late Mrs Ann Skewes, for the purposes of school assignment." Penzance, Cornwall. (no date)

Lloyd, Vera. "Timber Corps Diary: A personal account of working as a wood measurer and sub-forewoman at Boyton, outside Launceston, Cornwall." (no date)

Mason, Jeanne. "My Life in the Women's Timber Corps 1943-1947." 2005.

Ministry of Food. "One-pot Meals, Menus for 7 Days of the Week." 1945.

Ministry of Information. "Land at War: The official story of British farming 1939-1944." 1945.

Mist, Ellen. "Aw-Arrh! Experiences in the Women's Land Army." Cornwall: United Writers, 1992.

Mount, Isobel. "Miss Baxter and I," reprinted from *The Land Girl*, illustrated by the author. A series of articles bound in illustrated cover. (no date)

Nicholls, Mrs Elizabeth. "A Blackley Girl in Cornwall." A series in four parts. *Middleton Guardian*, Lancashire, 1980.

Oats, D. C. "Winter Diary: If winter comes, can spring be far behind?" Handwritten diary of WLA No 34895, 1942-43. Her first posting was a farm in Cornwall but by 1942-43 she had also been in Devon and was then posted to Walliswood Farm in Surrey.

Opie, Robert. "The Wartime Scrapbook on the Home Front: 1939 to 1945." Pi Global Publishing, 2005.

Parker, Pat. "Pat Parker's War." Unpublished diary. London, 1995.

War Pictures by British Artists, Women. Second Series, No 1. Oxford University Press, 1943.

Wartime News (2005 issue). Journal of the Wartime Company, P.O. Box 1939, Bournemouth BH1 1WT.

The *Western Morning News.* "The Land Girls (Land Girl Memories)," a 1998 series contributed by readers of the newspaper who talked to a large team of reporters about their wartime experiences. Series reporters included Jo Bishop, Colin Bradley, Su Carroll, Mark Clough, Robert Caruth, Chris Ferris, David Green, Colin Gregory, William Holman, Robert Jobson, Martyn Oates, Denise O'Leary, Clara Penn, Andrew Porter, Gloria Schofield, Noel Sliney, Ollie Stone-Lee, Michael Taylor and Mark Townsend.

MORE MEMORIES? WRITE THEM DOWN!